How to u

C000160707

In this issue

The 90 daily readings in this issue of *Explore* are designed to help you understand and apply the Bible as you read it each day.

It's serious!

We suggest that you allow 15 minutes each day to work through the Bible passage with the notes. It should be a meal, not a snack! Readings from other parts of the Bible can throw valuable light on the study passage. These cross-references can be skipped if you are already feeling full up, but they will expand your grasp of the Bible. *Explore* uses the NIV Bible translation, but you can also use it with the ESV or another translation of your choice.

Sometimes a prayer section will encourage you to stop and pray through the application of God's word—but it is always important to allow time to pray for God's Spirit to bring his word to life, and to shape the way we think and live.

We're serious!

All of us who work on *Explore* share a passion for getting the Bible into people's lives. We passionately hold to the Bible as God's word—to honour and follow, not to explain away.

1 Find a time you can read the Bible each day

2 Find a place where you can be quiet and think

3 Ask God to help you understand

4 Carefully read through the Bible passage for today

5 Study the verses with Explore, taking time to think

6 Pray about what you have read

thegoodbook
COMPANY

Opening up the Bible

Welcome to Explore

Being a Christian isn't a skill you learn, like carpentry or flower arranging. Nor is it a lifestyle choice, like the kind of clothes you wear, or the people you choose to hang out with. It's about having a real relationship with the living God through his Son, Jesus Christ. The Bible tells us that this relationship is like a marriage.

It's important to start with this, because many Christians view the practice of daily Bible-reading as a Christian duty, or a hard discipline that is just one more thing to get done in our busy modern lives.

But the Bible is God speaking to us: opening his mind to us on how he thinks, what he wants for us and what his plans are for the world. And most importantly, it tells us what he has done for us in sending his Son, Jesus Christ, into the world. It's the way the Spirit shows Jesus to us, and changes us as we behold his glory.

The Bible is not a manual. It's a love letter. And as with any love letter, we'll want to treasure it, and make time to read and Re-read it, so we know we are loved, and discover how we can please the One who loves us. Here are a few suggestions for making your daily time with God more of a joy than a burden:

- *Time:* Find a time when you will not be disturbed, and when the cobwebs are cleared from your mind. Many people have found that the morning is the best time as it sets you up for the day. If you're not a "morning person", then last thing at night or a mid-morning break might suit you. Whatever works for you is right for you.

- *Place:* Jesus says that we are not to make a great show of our religion *(see Matthew 6:5-6)*, but rather, to pray with the door to our room shut. Some people plan to get to work a few minutes earlier and get their Bible out in an office or some other quiet corner.

- *Prayer:* Although *Explore* helps with specific prayer ideas from the passage, try to develop your own lists to pray through. Use the flap inside the back cover to help with this. And allow what you read in the Scriptures to shape what you pray for yourself, the world and others.

- *Share:* As the saying goes: *expression deepens impression.* So try to cultivate the habit of sharing with others what you have learned. Why not join our Facebook group to share your encouragements, questions and prayer requests? Search for *Explore: For your daily walk with God.*

And remember, *it's quality, not quantity, that counts:* better to think briefly about a single verse than to skim through pages without absorbing anything. It's about developing your relationship with the Living God. The sign that your daily time with God is real is when you start to love him more and serve him more wholeheartedly.

Tim Thornborough and Carl Laferton
Editors

ROMANS: The new way

The gospel is a liberation story abut the dawning of an era of grace. But how does this new story connect with the older story of God's law? Paul starts to explain…

In the last issue in Romans 5 – 6 we saw that humanity in Adam is under the reign of sin which leads to death. But our old self (our old humanity) has died with Christ. So we're now under the reign of grace which leads to life. Now in chapter 7 Paul expands on what he said in Romans 5:20: "The law was brought in so that the trespass might increase") and in 6:14: "you are not under the law, but under grace").

When the law was given to humanity in Adam it did two things.

Sin increased
Read Romans 7:5

We inherited a rebellious attitude towards God from Adam (5:12). The law provoked this into acts of deliberate disobedience. The law told us what pleases God. But, because we hated God, we used the law to do what displeases God.

···· TIME OUT ··

Read Romans 4:15; 5:13 and 5:20 and see how these verses fit this picture.

Death sentence
Read Romans 3:19-20

The law not only revealed our sin, it also revealed the sentence of our sin = death.

Read Romans 7:1-3

❷ *What is Paul's point in these verses?*

❷ *How does it apply to Christians?*

In everyday life we know that death releases us from obligations. It's the same for Christians: we died with Christ and therefore we're free from the law. This means…

Read Romans 7:4

❷ *What has happened to a Christian believer and what for?*

We're freed from our death sentence. Sin no longer has any claim on us, since we belong to Christ. Paul highlights the fact that Jesus was raised from the dead. His resurrection is the guarantee of our resurrection. To die to the law means to die to the death sentence it demands. We are now to bear fruit.

Read Romans 7:6

We're being freed from our rebellious attitude. The old written code couldn't change us. In fact, it made matters worse. But, through the work of the Spirit, God's generous grace gives us a new desire to please God.

⌃ Pray

As you start 2021, make these gospel truths the centre of your prayerful commitment:

Praise God for your freedom from death and the crushing demands of the law.

Pray that you would live a fruitful, Spirit-directed life this year.

Law: what is it good for?

The law failed to make us right with God. So what's the point of it at all?

In Romans 5:20 Paul says that sin leads to grace. Then in chapter 6 he responds to the false conclusion that it's ok to sin. In 5:20 Paul also says that the law *leads* to sin (by provoking our rebellious attitude). So in chapter 7 he responds to the false conclusion that the law is bad.

The law: good at its job

❓ *What attitudes do people have to civil and religious or ethical laws today?*

Read Romans 7:7

❓ *What is Paul's point here?*

The law tells us what God requires. It therefore enables us to see that we're guilty and we need a Saviour.

The wrong tool

Read Romans 7:8-13

❓ *What is Paul's argument here?*
❓ *Do you recognise his description of how law provokes sin in your life?*

A hammer is good at driving nails. But imagine you've cut your finger and decide the best solution is to hit it with a hammer! You would soon discover that a hammer is very bad at healing wounds. That's not the hammer's fault. It's your fault for using it in the wrong way.

The law was good at its job of exposing our need and pointing to Jesus. But in the hands of sin, the law made matters worse. That wasn't the law's fault—the law is holy, righteous and good (v 12). But sin used the law to:

- provoke our rebellious attitude (v 8-9).
- proclaim our death sentence (v 10-11, 13).

Imagine a school child who hates his teacher. One day his teacher forbids chewing gum in class. Previously the boy had no desire to chew gum. But now he longs to do so, if only to annoy his teacher. Her "law" against chewing gum has provoked his rebellious attitude.

✓ Apply

The Old Testament law, as it has been fulfilled in Christ, helps us understand the richness and depth of God's will. It teaches us how we should live as Christians to please our heavenly Father. But keeping the law doesn't work as a way of becoming right with God (as we saw in chapter 3). And keeping the law on its own doesn't work as a way of becoming holy. The law can tell us what holiness looks like, but it can't motivate us to live holy lives. For that we need the heart-warming, heart-winning grace of God and the life-transforming work of the Spirit. We obey what the law says not because the law compels us, but because we want to please our Saviour.

What the law can't do…

The law is good at exposing our need and pointing to Jesus. But we also need to recognise what the law cannot do.

Frustrated Christians?

Read Romans 7:14-24

❷ *Who do you think these verses are describing: a believer or a non-believer?*
❷ *Which parts of this description resonate with your experience now and in the past?*

These verses see-saw backwards and forwards between a desire to do good and an inability to do good because of the presence and power of sin. Many people think Paul is describing a Christian who is frustrated by the way they still fall into sin. This may be correct, but if we compare verse 14 with 6:17-18, another possibility emerges. Perhaps Romans 7 is describing how we're still under the *influence* of sin, while Romans 6 is talking about how we're set free from the *authority* of sin. But it's hard to see how Paul could say we're no longer slaves of sin in chapter 6 and then say we're still slaves of sin in chapter 7.

So who else might Paul be talking about? In Romans 6 Paul has retold the story of the exodus: Christ has set us free from the slavery of sin just as Moses set Israel free from slavery of Egypt. Now in chapters 7 – 8 we continue that journey to Mount Sinai. Perhaps Paul is describing the relationship of a faithful Israelite's relationship to the law. As a believer he wants to obey God (he delights in God's law in 7:22). But without the Spirit writing God's law on his heart,

he's inevitably frustrated. So chapter 7 describes the problem for which the gift of the Spirit described in chapter 8 is the solution.

The law was good at its job of exposing our need and pointing to Jesus. What it could never do was to save us from the penalty and power of sin. For that we need Jesus and the Spirit.

The problem resolved

Read Romans 7:25 – 8:4

❷ *How do Jesus and the Spirit solve the problems posed in Romans 7?*

✓ Apply

Christians need to be disciplined in the battle against sin—offering every part of our lives to God (6:13). But rules, routines and willpower on their own cannot make us holy. That would be to live like an Old Testament believer. Instead:

• we constantly need to renew our vision of grace so our hearts are moved by love to obey God's word.

• we constantly need to depend on the work of the Spirit and pray for his help.

⌃ Pray

Talk to the Lord about your struggle with sin and how you seek to solve it.

The Spirit gives life

We ended chapter 7 feeling frustrated at humanity's inability to do what is good. In chapter 8 we burst into the new life that the Spirit brings.

Read Romans 8:1-4

❷ *What could the law not do?*
❷ *What has Jesus done?*
❷ *What is the Spirit doing?*

The law could tell us the life God requires, but it couldn't make us right with God, nor could it transform our sinful nature (our "flesh"). But Jesus satisfied the law's demands when he died in our place. So for us there is no condemnation (we are right with God). And the Spirit transforms us by giving us new life.

⌃ Pray

When do you feel like a failure? When do you feel condemned? Bring those situations to God in faith and hear God's words to you today: "There is now no condemnation for those who are in Christ Jesus".

Spirit life now
Read Romans 8:5-8

❷ *List the characteristics of those governed by the flesh.*
❷ *List the characteristics of those governed by the Spirit.*

The "flesh" is the sinful nature. It governs the lives of unbelievers. But, while Christians still feel its pull, we also enjoy the life-giving power of the Holy Spirit.

These verses are not a list of commands.

They're a description of an unbeliever (governed by the flesh) and a believer (governed by the Spirit). So if you're a Christian, hear these words as a promise. This is the life God has given you through the Spirit: you *can* please God.

Spirit life in the future
Read Romans 8:9-11

❷ *Who has the Spirit?*
❷ *What does the Spirit give?*
❷ *How can we be confident we'll be raised to eternal life after our physical death?*

The Spirit gives spiritual life in the present to every believer and this enables us to please God. This spiritual life is also a sign that God will give us physical life (resurrection) in the future. The Spirit unites us to Christ so *Christ's* resurrection becomes a promise of *our* resurrection.

⌄ Apply
Read Romans 8:12-13

The flesh (our sinful nature) still pulls us towards sin while the Spirit pulls us towards holiness. Our job is to follow the lead of the Spirit.

❷ *How are you feeling the pull of the flesh today?*
❷ *How are you feeling the pull of the Spirit today?*
❷ *Whose lead are you going to follow?*

The Spirit gives love

Have you ever prayed and felt that God has heard your prayers? Then you've experienced a mighty miracle. You've experienced the amazing power of the Holy Spirit.

Sons and lovers

Read Romans 8:14-15

- ❷ *What remarkable promises are there in these verses?*
- ❷ *Which one particularly excites you today?*
- ❷ *How important do you consider your feelings to be, as a Christian?*

In Romans 6 Paul has retold the exodus story. Just as Moses liberated Israel from the slavery of Egypt, so Jesus has liberated Christians from the slavery of sin. In Romans 7 we came to Mount Sinai to relive Israel's experience of the law. God led Israel by the pillars of cloud and fire to meet him at Mount Sinai. "When the people saw the thunder and lightning and heard the trumpet and saw the mountain in smoke, they trembled with fear. They stayed at a distance" (Exodus 20:18).

Now Christians are led by the Spirit to meet God. At this point we might well tremble with fear and keep our distance (like the Israelites). But we don't because the Spirit testifies that we're God's children.

- **Jesus makes us children of God.** Because we're in Christ we share his relationship with God the Father.
- **The Spirit makes us feel like children of God.** He gives us the confidence to come to God.

⌄ Apply

The Spirit wants us to stop living like slaves and start living like children.

- ❷ *How does a slave behave around their master?*
- ❷ *How does a child behave around their father?*

Read Romans 8:16-17

- ❷ *So what are the privileges of being a child of God?*
- ❷ *Which particularly excites you today?*

We can pray. Every prayer is a mighty miracle. Creatures ought to shrink in fear before their holy Creator. But we come to God in trusting, intimate prayer—often without giving it a second thought—because the Spirit powerfully testifies that God is our Father and that he delights to hear his children pray.

We will inherit. Children normally share in the family's wealth and the same is true for the children of God. Suffering is a normal part of the Christian life (as we'll see in the rest of chapter 8). But sharing Christ's suffering is a sign that we'll share his glory.

⌃ Pray

- ❷ *What are you going to say to your Father today?*

The Spirit gives hope

Our culture wants everything now. But one fruit of the Spirit is patience.

The renewal of creation
Read Romans 8:18-21

❓ *What is the present experience of creation?*
❓ *What will be its future experience?*

Creation was cursed when humanity sinned (Genesis 3:17-19). Plus our sin and greed harm the planet through things like global warming and pollution. But Christ will make all things new. Just as Christians will receive resurrection bodies, so the environment will be restored.

We're not there yet
Read Romans 8:22-25

❓ *Who groans in these verses?*
❓ *What does this look like in practice?*
❓ *What's the role of the Spirit in this?*

"Are we nearly there yet?" small children ask—just ten minutes into a seven-hour car journey. The groaning of creation and believers is the equivalent of this: "Are we nearly home in glory?" The answer is *not yet*—otherwise we wouldn't be looking forwards in hope (v 24-25).

The Spirit is the "firstfruits" of the new creation (v 23). Imagine having a spoonful of the rich gravy from a casserole while it's still cooking— you can't eat the main course yet, but it's a foretaste of the feast to come. The life and love the Spirit gives are a foretaste of the new creation.

✓ Apply

Sometimes people say, "You can be healed if you have enough faith". It's true we'll all be healed. *But not yet.* The full redemption of our bodies comes only when Christ returns and we're not there yet. In the meantime, suffering is a normal part of life (v 17-18) and so we wait patiently (v 25).

Read Romans 8:26-27

❓ *Who groans in these verses?*
❓ *What's the role of the Spirit here?*

The Spirit is with us when we feel the brokenness of a world that's not yet made new. When we don't know what to say, the Spirit prays for us and his prayers are always answered because they perfectly match God's will. And here is God's will for us...

Read Romans 8:28-30

❓ *How does God use suffering?*
❓ *How does God guarantee our future?*

God planned your salvation from before time (when he predestined you) right through to eternity (when you'll share Christ's glory). Along the way he uses *everything* that happens to make you more like Jesus.

✓ Apply

Think about your day. Receive every circumstance as a gift from God given to make you more like Jesus.

Bible in a year: Genesis 16-17 • Romans 6

All-conquering love

How do you know God loves you? What about when you get a cancer diagnosis or lose your job? What about when your sin accuses you or doubts dog your mind?

In this passage Paul asks four questions to reassure us of God's love.

Who can be against us?
Read Romans 8:31-32

- ❓ *When might you find yourself asking this question?*
- ❓ *What's the answer?*

If God gave us his precious Son then there can be no end or limit to his love. People may oppose us and circumstances may appear against us, but they *cannot* overcome God's love for us.

Who will bring a charge?
Read Romans 8:33

- ❓ *When might you find yourself asking this question?*
- ❓ *What's the answer?*

Perhaps I can separate myself from God by my sin. *No*, says Paul. You're not made right with God by what you do or don't do. It's God who justifies (makes us right with him) and nothing can undo that work.

Who condemns?
Read Romans 8:34

- ❓ *When might you find yourself asking this question?*
- ❓ *What's the answer?*

Who could rightly condemn us? Only Jesus. And Jesus is the very person who died to make us right with God. Far from bringing charges against us, Jesus is, in fact, interceding for us. He counters any accusation against us by presenting his finished work in the court of heaven.

Who shall separate us?
Read Romans 8:35-39

- ❓ *When might you find yourself asking this question?*
- ❓ *What's the answer?*

Sin cannot separate us from God's love, because God first demonstrated his love when we were sinners (5:8). Suffering cannot separate us, because we conquer suffering "through him who loved us". The past tense here is a reference to the cross. The cross is the great demonstration of God's love— even when our circumstances confuse us. Not even death can separate us, because God has given us eternal life through the resurrection of Jesus.

⌃ Pray

Bring to God the guilt of your sin and the confusion created by your suffering.

Pray through this passage verse by verse, applying it to your specific situation.

Praise God for his all-conquering love.

Together in Christ

So far in Romans Paul has described how, even though every one of us is guilty before God, we can be right with God through faith in Christ.

We no longer belong to the old humanity in Adam under the authority of sin and death. Instead, we've risen with Christ to live a new life in the power of the Spirit. If you are a Christian, this is who you are as you start out in 2021.

Paul has been concerned to show that this is the fulfilment of the Old Testament story. This is not some new idea made up by Paul; it was God's plan from the very beginning. Chapters 9 – 11 tackle this subject head on as Paul considers the place of the Jewish people in God's purposes.

My own race

Read Romans 9:1-5

> ❓ *Why does Paul feel anguish in his heart?*
> ❓ *What privileges do the Jewish people enjoy?*
> ❓ *Is Christianity antisemitic?*

Paul feels a deep love for his fellows Jews. But that love takes the form of *anguish* because many Jews are missing out on the good news of Jesus the Messiah. The exodus, covenants, law, temple, and all the rich heritage and history they have all pointed to the coming of Jesus as the Messiah (as Paul has shown in chapters 1 – 8). But they have rejected him.

God's true people

Read Romans 9:6-9

> ❓ *To what accusation is Paul responding?*
> ❓ *Who are the true people of God?*

If many Jews are missing out on salvation, then have God's promises failed? *No*, says Paul. God is saving his people as promised, but the people he is saving are not defined by ethnicity.

In verse 6 Paul uses the term "Israel" in two senses: "Israel" = the ethnic people of Israel and "Israel" = the true people of God. Not all the ethnic group belong to the true people of God. What matters is faith in Christ.

Paul's reasoning reminds us that Abraham had many sons. So being a descendant of Abraham is not enough. In fact, being a descendant of Isaac (Abraham's son according to the promise) is not enough. What matters is what Isaac represents: faith in God's promises—the promises fulfilled in Jesus. Chapter 11 says that Gentiles believers have also been added to God's people. So God's people = believing Jews + believing Gentiles.

···· TIME OUT ·······································

Read Galatians 4:21-31

> ❓ *How does Paul use the same kind of argument here as he does in Romans 9:7-9?*

⌃ Pray

Pray for the Jewish people. Ask God to bring many Jews to faith in Jesus.

By him who calls

Why are you a Christian? "Because I've put my faith in Christ," you might respond. Correct. That's what we see in Romans 3 – 4. But that raises a further question…

Why did you put your faith in Christ? "Because the Spirit opened my eyes," you explain. But guess what? That raises yet *another* question: *Why did the Spirit open your eyes? Did you do something that made you worthy to receive his new life?* Paul answers this sticky question like this: "Not by works but by him who calls" (Romans 9:12).

Read Romans 9:10-13

Two generations after Abraham, the blessing of being God's true people skipped the eldest son (Esau) and passed instead to the younger son (Jacob). What had Jacob done to deserve this? *Nothing.* We can be sure it had nothing to do with merit because God announced this before the two boys had even been born (v 11).

Ultimately the blessing of belonging to God's true people doesn't depend on what *we* do but on *God's* choice—what Paul calls "God's purpose in election". Note that love and hate in 12:13 are not emotions God feels, but the results of his actions—blessing to Jacob instead of Esau, belonging to God's people and not belonging.

"But how can this be fair?" you might ask. Good question. Paul addresses it head on.

Read Romans 9:14-15

- ❷ *What is God's idea of fairness?*

For us justice = eternal condemnation, for that's what we really deserve (as we see in Romans 1 – 3). If justice were the only

consideration, then we would all be lost. But God is also merciful, and in his mercy he chose to save some (and remain just by condemning Jesus in our place at the cross, as we saw in 3:23-26).

Read Romans 9:16-18

- ❷ *How certain would our salvation be if it depended on human desire or effort?*
- ❷ *What difference does it make to know that our salvation depends on God's mercy?*
- ❷ *What is the result of election, according to verse 17?*

If salvation depended on human desire or effort, then we would all be lost for ever. Because it depends on God's mercy, then those whom God chooses are saved, for sure, for ever.

TIME OUT

Read Exodus 4:21 and 8:15

- ❷ *Who hardens Pharaoh's heart? What does this suggest about the relationship between God's sovereignty and human responsibility?*

⌄ Apply

Read Acts 18:9-11

- ❷ *How does election motivate evangelism?*
- ❷ *What difference will this make to your prayers and your life this week?*

I get knocked down…

We may not be physically persecuted as Christians in the West (yet), but the world is increasingly hostile to Christian values. What happens when we get knocked down?

What do you expect?
Read Proverbs 24:15

❷ *What kind of persecution can a Christian experience today:*
  - *in countries around the world?*
  - *closer to your home?*
❷ *What are the two instructions the "unrighteous" receive in verse 15?*

The language of being plundered conjures up images of a thief lurking in the bushes, awaiting his chance to break and enter, and ransack the building—sadly, a common occurrence in many countries today.

❷ *What is the command to "the righteous" person (someone who is right with God through faith in Jesus Christ) in v 15?*
❷ *What might a righteous person expect in life today (v 15)?*
❷ *Can you think of any examples where Christians have been attacked, their homes destroyed or their lives ruined on account of violent people wanting to see their downfall?*

Jesus never promised an easy life for his followers. There are Christians who feel this pressure acutely today. And if we personally don't experience this kind of persecution, we can be sure that is not the norm. Christians remain heavily persecuted worldwide, even though in the Western world we have experienced relative freedom from such aggression in recent times.

TIME OUT

Read John 15:18-25

❷ *What comfort can being chosen (v 19) give you:*
  - *when ridiculed for your faith?*
  - *when it seems the wicked are prosperous?*

… but I get up again
Read Proverbs 24:16

❷ *What assurance can a righteous person enjoy?*

The number seven in the Bible symbolises completeness. A Christian can be completely sure that the wicked will *never* win, but will ultimately stumble and fall. By contrast, despite the innumerable times that a Christian might get knocked down because of our faith, we will not remain down. Our pattern here is the one we follow. Our Lord Jesus fell at the hands of the wicked, but heroes again. In Christ we see God's promises fulfilled.

⌃ Pray

Pray that you would stand firm in the face of persecution. Pray for Christians who are in the midst of persecution today, and for their abusers and attackers to heed God's warning.

Bible in a year: Genesis 25-26 • Romans 9:1-15

The riches of his glory

Why did God create a world that would end in judgment for some people? We can't fully know the answer. But Paul gives a hint…

The rights of God

Read Romans 9:19-21

> ❓ *What's the accusation being made against God?*
> ❓ *How does Paul respond to this accusation?*

God and humanity are not equals. We cannot sit in judgment on God's plans. He is the eternal Creator, and we are his finite creatures. There is an infinite gulf between us. That means:

- we have no right to judge our Creator.
- God has every right to do what he wants with his creatures.

····· TIME OUT ·································

Paul alludes to a visit that the prophet Jeremiah made to the potter's house.

Read Jeremiah 18:1-6

> ❓ *How do these verses reinforce Paul's point in Romans 9:19-21?*

The glory of God

Read Romans 9:22-23

Paul's argument is this: God has chosen to allow some people to remain in their sin so the rightness or righteousness of his judgment might be evident. (Even though these people deserve wrath, God has shown great patience towards them in delaying that wrath.) God has chosen other people (who also deserve wrath) to be saved through his mercy. Why has God planned things in this way? "To make the riches of his glory known." Only when we see God's judgment in action do we understand the depths of his grace and the wonder of our salvation.

> ❓ *How do you feel about Paul's explanation here?*
> ❓ *What questions remain for you as you grapple with this teaching?*

⌃ Pray

Thank God for his patience towards our rebellious world and thank him for his saving mercy towards you.

The mission of God

Read Romans 9:24-29

This section on the mission of God is part of Paul's explanation of why God's promises to Israel have not failed (v 6). It was always God's plan to call both Jews and Gentiles to be his people (v 24). The prophets said that God would include Gentiles (v 25-26) and save only a remnant of Jews (v 27-29). So God's promises have not failed: quite the opposite.

- By saving Jews by faith God has fulfilled his promise to save a remnant.
- By saving Gentiles by faith God has fulfilled his promise to bring blessing to all nations.

Christ is near

God has fulfilled his promises by saving both some Jews and some Gentiles by faith in Christ.

Is that right, Paul? Even though that means irreligious Gentiles are right with God ("have obtained righteousness") while religious Jews miss out? *Spot on,* says Paul...

Read Romans 9:30-33

Paul's not talking about every Gentile here, but about those with faith in Christ. Nor is he talking about every Jew, but only about those without faith (see 10:16). The focus is on these two groups because Paul is addressing two questions:

- *How come some Jews are missing out on salvation (9:6)?*
  Answer: Because they're trying to be right with God through law-keeping, which never works.
- *How come some Gentiles are being included in salvation?*
  Answer: Because they're right with God by faith in Christ.

"But surely many Jews are extremely devout? Do they *really* miss out on salvation?"

Read Romans 10:1-4

Yes, devout people can miss out, says Paul. Zeal is only good if it's zeal for the right things. Imagine you need to cross a river. There's a bridge which represents Christ. The best option is confidently to walk across the bridge (to trust in Christ). But if the choice is between hesitantly walking over the bridge or confidently attempting to jump, then hesitant faith is best. No amount of passion will save you if that passion is misplaced. And the river is so wide that no one can possibly jump across.

It's easy to be intimidated by religious people. But are they proudly trying to establish their own righteousness or are they humbly submitting to God's righteousness (v 3)?

Read Romans 10:5-13

❓ *How do we not draw near to Christ?*
❓ *How do we draw near to Christ?*

We don't have work our way up to God or discover Christ in the depths through spiritual exercises or moral endeavour. Instead, Christ comes near to us through his word. All we need to do is trust that word and entrust ourselves to Christ. So ultimately Gentiles and Jews are in exactly the same situation: "there is no difference" (v 12). Whoever you are, you can be saved by calling on the name of Jesus.

Re-read Romans 10:9

❓ *Paul gives us two things to do. How are they alike? What does declaring with our mouth add to believing in our heart?*

☑ Apply

❓ *Every time God's word is read or preached, Christ is near. How should that shape your attitude to reading our Bibles and listening to preaching?*

The logic of mission

People need Christ. But how do they get him? Salvation doesn't require some heroic task we must complete.

We don't need to reach new heights or explore profound depths Romans 10:6-7). The hero is Jesus, and Jesus comes near through God's word. The benefits of Jesus are conveyed through his word when people respond with faith (v 8-9). This truth creates an important piece of missionary logic.

The need to hear

Read Romans 10:13-15

> ❓ *What's the chain of cause and effect in these verses?*

Follow the logic in the steps below:

- People are saved by calling on Christ's name (v 13).
- To call on Christ's name people must believe in him (v 14).
- To believe in him people must hear about him (v 14).
- To hear about him someone must tell them (v 14).
- For someone to tell others they must be sent (v 15).
- God has sent us to tell others about Christ (v 15).

The conclusion is this: if people are going to be saved, then we must obey God's call to speak. "How beautiful are the feet of those who bring good news" is our commission! God says it's a beautiful thing when we tell people about Jesus.

✅ Apply

By speaking of "preaching" here, Paul doesn't just mean delivering a sermon. He means any communication of the gospel using words—a conversation, a Bible study, an invitation, an email.

> ❓ *What could you do to tell someone about Jesus today?*

More than hearing

Hearing about Jesus is vital if people are going to be saved. But hearing is not enough.

Read Romans 10:16-21

Paul is considering why some Jews miss out on salvation. Was the problem that they failed to hear? *No*, they saw God in creation and heard his word in the Old Testament Scriptures. (This is what Psalm 19, quoted in verse 18, teaches.) So was the problem that God's word failed (9:6)? No, it's not a failure of God's word as God's word is powerful to save (10:13). It was a failure to respond with faith.

🔼 Pray

To whom might you speak of Jesus today? Pray that God would give them faith as they hear the word.

A faithful remnant

Paul was a Jew through and through with a passion for the salvation of his people. But a difficult question hung over him.

Read Romans 11:1

❓ *What's question does Paul anticipate?*

Paul anticipates this question because he's just said many Jews are missing out on being right with God (9:31-33). So have they been replaced in God's affections by Gentiles (9:30)?

Read Romans 11:1-6

❓ *What's the answer Paul gives?*

Paul's answer is an emphatic *No!* God is still committed to Jews. *But what's the proof?*

- **Exhibit A:** *Paul himself*
  Paul is a Jew who is now right with God through faith in Christ.

- **Exhibit B:** *Elijah*
  The prophet Elijah spoke for God at the time when King Ahab was leading the people of Israel in the worship of Baal. Elijah once complained that he was all on his own—no one else was faithful to God. But it wasn't true. God was able to point to 7,000 faithful Israelites.

···· TIME OUT ····

Read the story of Elijah's complaint for yourself in 1 **Kings 19:1-18** and reflect on God's responses.

Paul describes those Jews who trust in Christ as "a remnant" (Romans 11:5). It's a word the Old Testament prophets often used. As they condemned the Israelites for their infidelity towards God, they also said that a faithful remnant would remain who would become God's true people. Paul says that this promise is being fulfilled in the church—made up of both Jews *and* Gentiles who are faithful because they have faith in Christ.

But ultimately the remnant is not a sign of human faithfulness but of divine faithfulness. Remnant people are "chosen by grace" (v 5). They are not saved by their faithfulness to God but by his grace (v 6).

Read Romans 11:7-10

God allowed those who rejected his grace to become hardened in their sin. But in his grace he chose some: his elect. The word "elect" in verse 7 is the same word as "chosen" in verse 5. God chose to renew and reshape their hearts so that they turned to him in faith. This is what happens when someone becomes a Christian—whether Jew or Gentile. Before we can please God, the Holy Spirit must give us new life and new desires, as Paul says in Romans 8:5-8.

☑ Apply

Do you feel alone in your home or workplace? Does your church seem to be alone in your neighbourhood? Remember that God has his elect there, chosen by grace. At some point, when they hear the gospel (perhaps for the hundredth time), they will respond with Spirit-given faith.

Wild branches

Is there still hope for the Jewish people? Yes, says Paul. In the present, Jewish people are being saved by faith in Christ. And in the future many more may be saved…

The story isn't over yet
Read Romans 11:11-16

❓ *What's the question that Paul anticipates people asking?*
❓ *How does he answer it?*

The rejection of Jesus by many Jews means that the gospel has gone out beyond Judaism to the Gentiles (v 11). That's what happened in miniature in Paul's own ministry. When he arrived in a new city, he would start preaching in the synagogue. Only when he was thrown out would he go the Gentiles.

So the rejection of the gospel by Jews led to blessing for Gentiles. Paul then invites us (v 12, 15) to imagine what blessing the inclusion of Jews might lead to! Perhaps Paul has in mind a worldwide revival.

In the meantime, Paul takes the gospel message to Gentiles in the hope that their inclusion might arouse Jews to come to God through faith in Jesus (v 13-14). "Christian" means "belonging to the Christ" or to the Messiah. Christianity is therefore a constant reminder to Judaism of its Messiah.

Don't be arrogant
Read Romans 11:17-21

At this point Paul's Gentile readers (including many of us) might be feeling pretty smug, since God has accepted us (albeit by grace rather than any merit in us).

❓ *How does Paul counter any sense of superiority?*

Even in its current state of rejection, Judaism as a corporate entity continues to have a special place in the story of salvation. Individual unbelieving Jews may be like broken off branches (v 17), but Judaism as a corporate entity continues to be the holy root from which God's people (believing Jews and Gentiles) have grown (v 16). God has not replaced Judaism with the church, but continued Judaism *within* the church. This is why Paul has been at pains to underline that we can never boast in ourselves but only in Christ (see 3:27-28 and 5:1-5)

Gospel hope
Read Romans 11:22-24

The story of Israel shouldn't make us feel smug. Instead it should…

• make us rejoice in God's kindness to us.

• motivate us to remain faithful to God.

There's also hope here for evangelism among Jews: if God can graft wild branches (Gentiles) into his people, then he can re-graft cultivated branches (Jews). The story isn't over yet…

⌃ Pray

Pray for the work of evangelism among Jewish people.

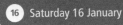
All Israel

These chapters talk a lot about the future of both Jews and Gentiles. The rejection of Judaism is neither total nor final. But what's really at stake is the character of God.

Can God be trusted? Can we trust his promises? Do his ways make sense?

Read Romans 11:25-27

> ❷ *What's the mystery that Paul is revealing to his readers?*
> ❷ *What do you think he means by the phrase "all Israel will be saved"?*

Paul has used "Israel" to mean both "ethnic Jews" and "God's true people" (= both believing Jews and believing Gentiles). Paul uses both senses in 9:6: "Not all who are descended from Israel are Israel". That is, not all Israel (ethnic Jews) are part of Israel (God's true people).

So in 11:26 "all Israel" could mean God's true people—Jews and Gentiles (2:28-29; 4:11-12 and Galatians 6:16). When the full number of Gentiles have been saved, then God's people will include people from every nation.

Or "all Israel" could mean ethnic Judaism. Paul could be saying that one day many Jews will be saved (the quotes in Romans 11:26-27 promise repentance and forgiveness) so that all the elect Jews or Judaism as a corporate entity will again be part of God's people.

Read Romans 11:28-32

At the moment unbelieving Jews are both enemies (when they oppose the gospel) and loved (because they're the holy root from which salvation came, v 16). The disobedience of the Jews serves to display God's mercy all the more clearly when he moves them to faith and repentance (v 31)— just as with everyone else (v 32).

Failed promises?

Paul's central claim in Romans is that we are right with God *only* by faith in Jesus. But many Jews have rejected faith in Jesus. Does this mean God's promises to Israel have failed?

- *No*, because God is free to choose who he saves (chapter 9).
- *No*, because the real problem is Israel's lack of faith (chapter 10).
- *No*, because God is saving Jews as they come to faith in Jesus (chapter 11).

Think back over what we have seen in Romans 9 – 11.

> ❷ *What have we seen that humbles you?*
> ❷ *What have we seen that excites you?*

▲ Pray

Read Romans 11:33-36

Turn these verses, one phrase at a time, into confession and praise.

When your enemy falls…

The verses today follow on from last Sunday's proverb, in which we saw the inevitable stumbling of the wicked.

God's heart
Read Proverbs 24:17

❓ *What are God's people specifically called not to do (v 17)?*

❓ *What is the difference between gloating over a person's downfall and being pleased that evil and wickedness have been stopped?*

❓ *Why does the proverb mention the "heart" in a person's response to such stumbling?*

The heart is a way of describing a person's desire. Thus, for a person's heart to find joy in the fall of a fellow sinful human shows up something dark within us that might feel natural but is far from God's desires.

TIME OUT

Read Ezekiel 33:11

❓ *What is God's desire?*

As Jesus hung on the cross, he prayed for his Father to forgive his executioners. What they were doing was heinous beyond comprehension, and would, without repentance, lead to eternal devastation. And yet Jesus did not gloat over how they would suffer but prayed for them. Jesus, the image of the invisible God, showed his heart for the lost.

❓ *When did you last pray for someone who had hurt you, or for someone you saw on the news who had done evil?*

❓ *How can you encourage yourself to make this a regular part of your prayer life?*

Vengeance is mine
Read Proverbs 24:18

❓ *What is the surprise in this verse?*

❓ *Who is it that brings justice ("wrath") on the wicked?*

❓ *What does this verse and Romans 12:17-21 encourage us to do, knowing that only the Lord has the right to avenge?*

We are to leave the how and the when to the Lord, who does not delight in the judgment of the wicked. In fact, leaving judgment to the Lord will show that we trust that he will punish justly. Gloating will show that we have not grasped that God will punish evil in his way, and may even result in God withholding judgment in order, presumably, to show us the error of our ways.

⌄ Apply

❓ *Do you need to repent of times when you have seen or heard about people who have met their downfall, and gloated? What can your response be going forward?*

⌃ Pray

Pray that your heart reflects God's own heart in the way you view evildoers.

In view of God's mercy

The gospel of Jesus brings with it obligations. But this is not where it begins.

Viewing God's mercy

Read Romans 12:1

What comes first is understanding God's mercy towards us. In Romans 12 Paul starts to describe how the church is to live. But we're already 11 chapters into the letter!

> ❓ *What have you learned about God's mercy to you so far in Romans?*

Those who are right with God through faith in Christ have a new future (chapters 1 – 4), have a new life (chapters 5 – 8) and belong to a new people (chapters 9 – 11). We don't earn this—it's by grace. But it has implications for how we live.

⌄ Apply

> ❓ *How can you keep God's mercy in view today? This week?*

Responding to mercy

Our response to God's mercy is to worship.

Re-read Romans 12:1

> ❓ *What are the characteristics of our worship in response to God's mercy?*

Our worship is:

- **bodily and "living"** = involving our whole lives
- **communal** = as all of us together offer "our bodies" (plural), we create a shared

life that is one singular sacrifice to God
- **"holy" (or consecrated) and "pleasing"** = we bring pleasure to God as we serve him
- **"true" or "spiritual"** (literally "rational") = the logical response to God's mercy.

⌄ Apply

> ❓ *What's the connection between our corporate worship on a Sunday and our living worship throughout the week?*
> ❓ *How should the first fuel the second?*

Renewing our minds

Read Romans 12:2

> ❓ *What does it mean to conform to the pattern of this world?*
> ❓ *What does it mean to renew our minds?*

Our transformation begins with our minds. This doesn't simply mean acquiring more information about God. It means a radical change in the way we think about everything. We stop thinking like the world around us and start thinking about life in the light of God's mercy.

We start to think of God as a loving Father rather than a harsh kill-joy. We think of being right with God as a gift rather than an attainment. And so we think of God's will as "good, pleasing and perfect" rather than as an unwelcome burden.

Think different

Who would you pick to be in your church or home group? Of course we don't get to pick; God does. And he's carefully selected the people in your church for your good.

Romans 12:2 has called on us to change our thinking, and immediately we are challenged to think in a different way about the people God has put us next to.

Read Romans 12:3

- ❓ *What do you think the phrase "sober judgment" means?*
- ❓ *What do you think Paul means by the "measure of faith" (ESV)?*

If your faith is stronger, it's because God gave you that measure of faith. It's not something to be proud of. Faith is not a substance we accumulate or a confidence we can summon in ourselves through our own effort. Faith is trusting in God. Big faith is simply the recognition that we have a big God. So we can't boast about having lots of faith; we can only boast in a big God.

☑ Apply

- ❓ *What measure of faith do you think you have been given?*
- ❓ *Think of two people who you think may have a greater or smaller measure of faith than you. How do you think of them?*

If you look down on other people, then you haven't understand how faith and grace work—so perhaps you're not as mature as you think!

Read Romans 12:4-6

- ❓ *What is Paul's big idea here, and what does he want us to do about it?*

The church is like a human body. Just as the body is made up of different limbs and organs with different functions, so a church is made up of many individuals with different roles. So our differences make us stronger and more effective—when we work together.

☑ Apply

- *We need you!* Your contribution may be different from that of other people, *but it matters.* So don't feel inferior.
- *You need us!* Your abilities are not better; they're just different. Plus your abilities are not your achievements—they're God's gifts given "according to the grace given to each of us". So don't feel superior.

Giving our all

Read Romans 12:6-8

There are two warnings implicit in this list. Don't complain that other people are not doing what you do. And don't complain that you can't do what others can do.

Church life is not a competition for roles or recognition. God's gifts are given not so we can be self-serving but self-giving. It is not about self-fulfilment but about building up others in the body of Christ.

Re-read Romans 12:8

- ❓ *Are you serving your church generously, diligently and cheerfully?*

A gorgeous gathering

Though sometimes the culture of a church can turn toxic, most of the time a local church is a beautiful thing.

There is nowhere else in your neighbourhood where such a diverse group of people come together as family. Paul paints a picture of this beautiful community life in today's reading.

Read Romans 12:9-16

Think about each of the characteristics of a beautiful church that Paul identifies. In each case consider these questions:

> ❓ *What does this characteristic look like in your church? (To clarify what each characteristic looks like, try to identify its opposite.)*
> ❓ *How could you better embody this characteristic?*

1. Love must be sincere.
2. Hate what is evil; cling to what is good.
3. Be devoted to one another in love.
4. Honour one another above yourselves.
5. Never be lacking in zeal, but keep your spiritual fervour, serving the Lord.
6. Be joyful in hope.
7. Be patient in affliction.
8. Be faithful in prayer.
9. Share with the Lord's people who are in need.
10. Practise hospitality.
11. Bless those who persecute you; bless and do not curse.
12. Rejoice with those who rejoice.
13. Mourn with those who mourn.
14. Live in harmony with one another.
15. Do not be proud, but be willing to associate with people of low position. Do not be conceited.

⌃ Pray

As you review the life of your church, pick three things for which you want to give thanks.

Pick three things you want to pray for and ask God to grow them—either in yourself or in your church.

⌄ Apply

Everything in these verses is a call to practical action. So knowing what we should do is clear. When it comes to application the big question is *how*? *How* do we love people from the heart? *How* do we hate evil when our culture often celebrates it? *How* do we honour others when we long to be acclaimed? *How* do we maintain our spiritual zeal? *How* can we be patient in affliction? *How* do we keep on praying when no answer seems to come? *How* can we bless people who are unkind to us? *How* can we live in harmony with people who annoy us? *How* can we avoid pride without feeling proud of our humility?

Re-read Romans 12:1-2

> ❓ *What answer to these questions can we find in verses 1-2?*

How can good beat evil?

Sooner or later everyone finds themselves wronged in some way. Usually these experiences are simply annoying and don't leave behind lasting harm.

But some people become victims of crime, bullying, betrayal or persecution. We are vulnerable people in a hostile world, and being a Christian can mean suffering from increased hostility. Suffering is part of being united to Christ (Romans 8:17).

Looking for trouble

Read Romans 12:17-18

- ❓ *We can't always avoid trouble, but how might we make it more likely or exacerbate it?*
- ❓ *What could you do "as far as it depends on you" to minimise conflict?*

Looking to bless

Read Romans 12:19-21

- ❓ *What should you not do?*
- ❓ *What should you do?*
- ❓ *How might you be tempted to take revenge?*

For some revenge means throwing punches or shouting abuse. But it can also involve doing as little as possible or withdrawing in a sulk (being "passive aggressive"). Others talk behind people's backs, taking revenge on a person's reputation.

Paul not only calls us to stop taking revenge but to start blessing those who persecute us—to "overcome evil with good". Verse 20 gives some practical examples of what this might involve.

- ❓ *How could you bless those who make your life difficult?*

Looking to God

It can be appropriate to turn to the relevant authorities when we're wronged (as we shall see in 13:1-7). But that doesn't always resolve the situation.

Re-read Romans 12:19

- ❓ *What's our ultimate hope for justice?*
- ❓ *How does this help us endure suffering now?*

God's justice will be done—if not in this life, then in the next. That's good news, unless you've ever been selfish or unkind —and that includes every one of us! The problem with crying out for vengeance is that we've all wronged other people.

God always avenges wrong. For unbelievers that takes place at the final judgment (Romans 2:5). For believers it has taken place at the cross. At the cross God justly avenged the wrong we have done by judging Jesus in our place (3:25-26). We can show mercy because we've received mercy (12:1).

⌃ Pray

Read Matthew 5:43-44

Here's one way to bless those who make life difficult for us—pray for them.

God's strange servants

How should Christians relate to the state? It's something that many Christians struggle with, but Paul gives some clear principles in today's passage.

Read Romans 13:1-7

❓ *Find all the commands in these verses.*
❓ *Now identify all the reasons for these commands.*

Submit to the state

We're to "be subject to the governing authorities" (v 1, 5). We're do what the state defines as right (v 3) and avoid what it defines as wrong (v 4). Verse 7 expands these principles to every level of society—including the police, civil servants, government agencies and schools.

Remember Paul himself had a run-in with the state on a number of occasions. He'd been arrested, beaten, and imprisoned simply for preaching the gospel. Yet he still commends submission to political authorities. *Why?*

The reasons

God has established the state. Three times in verses 1-2 Paul says the state is "established by God". Whether they recognise it or not, our politicians are God's servants (v 4, 6). So to rebel against the state is to rebel against God (v 2). By respecting authorities and paying taxes we're honouring God.

But there's another, practical, reason why we should submit: because the state punishes wrongdoers. In verses 3, 4 and 5 Paul says we should obey the state because otherwise we're likely to be fined or imprisoned. God in his kindness has given us the state to restrain evil. It may be difficult to grasp, but even a corrupt state is better than no state at all—anarchy.

So why should I, for example, obey the speed limit? First, the God reason. The police officer with the speed gun is God's servant, whom I should honour "as a matter of conscience" (v 5). Second, the practical reason. I may get fined for breaking the limit: "because of possible punishment" (v 5).

TIME OUT

But what about when the state is evil?

1. **Read Acts 5:29.** While we should obey the state whenever possible, we should disobey the state whenever necessary.

2. Compare Romans 12:19 and 13:4. While we should look to the state to avenge injustice on God's behalf, our ultimate hope for justice is God.

Pray

Pray that your political leaders would commend those who do right (v 3) and punish those who do wrong (v 4).

Read 1 Timothy 2:1-4

Pray that your political leaders would allow Christians to proclaim the gospel freely so that people might come to a knowledge of the truth.

The law of love

We often think of laws as an unwelcome restriction or a necessary evil. On the other hand, we think love is great. But law and love are really two sides of the same coin.

People of the law

Read Romans 13:7-8

Paul has just said we should give what we owe—whether that's taxes, revenue, respect or honour (v 7). Verse 8 sums it up: "Let no debt remain outstanding". But there is one obligation that never ends—the obligation to love one another.

Read Romans 13:9-10

Love is the summary and fulfilment of the law of Moses. Every other law is really an application of the command to love. Law is simply love getting down to earth.

···· TIME OUT ··

These verses help us read the Old Testament properly. The law of Moses described how Israel were to love God and one another in an agrarian economy before the coming of Christ. Our context is different—both our social context and our relationship to the coming of Christ. So we no longer obey many of the ceremonial and civil aspects of the law of Moses. But the law of love remains the same. Moreover, by showing what love required from the Israelites back then, the law of Moses can inform us as we work out what love requires from us today.

⌄ Apply

Read 1 John 3:16-18

- ❷ *What did love look like for Jesus?*
- ❷ *Is there someone today you could love with actions rather than simply with words?*

People of the day

Read Romans 13:11-14

Paul is talking here about the coming of a new world at the return of Christ. He describes our present age as "the night" and the coming of the new age as the dawning of "the day". He's playing on the idea that crimes and misdemeanours are often committed under the cover of darkness. Christians are to wake up and live as people of the day—behaving in a way that is consistent with God's coming new world.

- ❷ *What behaviours are we to avoid?*
- ❷ *What behaviours are we to adopt?*

Notice that verses 11-14 are all a rationale for the call to "do this" in verse 11, and "this" is the life of love described in verses 8-10.

⌃ Pray

Pray you would have the opportunity to show love to others today, both in big ways and in the small everyday interactions you have with them.

Fretting and fearing

Today we will see a call not to fret over the wicked but to fear those who can bring justice.

Evil effects
Read Proverbs 24:19-20

> ❷ *What are the instructions of verses 19?*
> ❷ *Who are these instructions for?*

Last week in verses 17-18, we were warned against one type of response to the inevitable downfall of the wicked: *gloating*. Today we are warned against two quite opposite responses to evildoers: *fretting*, or compulsive worrying, and *envy*.

> ❷ *Why might a believer "fret" or "be envious of the wicked" even when we know about their ultimate downfall?*

It is a part of how God has ordered his world that no sin is so personal that it does not affect others. So the effects of some wicked act might be felt for days, months or even a lifetime. You might be living now in the shadow of someone's sinful actions towards you personally, even if it was years ago and the perpetrator is long gone. However, there are two important truths to hold on to.

> ❷ *What is the encouragement (v 20)?*
> ❷ *Why is that sometimes difficult to believe?*

There will be no eternal reward for those who reject Christ, and their destination is not to be envied.

···· **TIME OUT** ··

Read Psalm 37

Evil's end
Read Proverbs 24:21-22

> ❷ *Who are we to fear?*
> ❷ *Why?*
> ❷ *What does verse 22 tell us about justice from the Lord and his delegated authorities?*

To fear God is not a cowering terror but a humility and submission to God as our divine authority. God delegates his authority to the king; and through the king, and the apparatus of state, he enacts his judgment on evil—or at least part of it.

> ❷ *Why should this help us not to "fret because of evildoers," or be "envious" and "join in" with rebelling against the Lord and his delegated authorities?*

☑ Apply

> ❷ *How does this encourage you to be a good citizen?*

☑ Pray

Praise God that you can trust him for justice, just as you can trust that the justice that we deserve to bear for our sins has been paid by Christ, our substitute, on the cross.

Pray for those who cry for justice. Pray that they would find peace in seeing that God is the ultimate judge and that justice will be served in this life or the next.

Bible in a year: Isaiah 7-9 • Mark 3:1-35

Church wars

It's a sad reality that many people view Christians as hopelessly divided and fond of picking fights with each other. So what should we do when we disagree?

When to let it go

Read Romans 14:1

We shouldn't quarrel over "disputable issues" or "opinions". A "disputable issue" is something over which Christians can disagree without compromising the gospel.

Read Romans 14:2-6

> ❷ *What were the disputable issues in Rome over which Christians should have agreed to disagree?*
> ❷ *Can you think of examples of disputable issues today over which Christians should agree to disagree?*

When to take a stand

Paul took an implacable stand against false teaching. Paul was even willing publicly to confront the apostle Peter in Galatians 2:11-14. There are clearly at least two scenarios when we may need to take a stand (even if that does mean "quarrelling").

1. When people reject the central truths of the faith. The New Testament is full of commands to oppose false teaching which undermines the message of salvation in Christ (see 1 Timothy 1:3-5).

2. When people turn secondary issues into primary issues. Paul saw circumcision as a secondary issue (Galatians 6:15), and he was happy to circumcise Timothy to help reach unbelieving Jews (Acts 16:1-3). But Paul refused to circumcise

Titus when people insisted that circumcision was a necessary part of being a Christian—that is, when people falsely made it a primary issue (Galatians 2:3).

No condemnation

Read Romans 14:4, 7-12

God is the master of other Christians—not you (v 4). They are to live to please the Lord, who died for them (v 7-9)—not to please you. Other Christians must stand before God to give an account (v 10-12)—so you shouldn't, as it were, make them stand before you to give an account.

What's more, God enables them to stand before him (v 4)—not necessarily because they're in the right but because they're in Christ (5:1-2). We must not condemn those for whom there is now no condemnation (8:1). Other Christians don't need to win your approval because they already have God's approval. We can live with differences because we all live "in view of God's mercy" (12:1).

🔼 Pray

Pray for those in your church with whom you disagree.

When right is wrong

Do you ever feel judged by other Christians? Do you ever judge others? It's tempting to want to be proved right. But Paul shows that there may be bigger issues at stake.

Loving your family
Read Romans 14:13-23

Look carefully at verses 14, 20 and 23. The same activity can be ok for one Christian and not for another. If someone is convinced something is wrong, then for them it *is* wrong. The activity itself may be ok, but if they think it's wrong and still do it, they're choosing to disobey God.

Now look carefully at verses 15 and 21-22. This means it can also be wrong for you to do this activity—even though you're (rightly) persuaded that it's ok.

Paul is clear that Christians are free to eat meat or not and keep the Sabbath or not. We tend to think of weak Christians as those who are not very strict or disciplined, but here the weak Christians are the over-strict ones, who don't fully understand the freedom they have in Christ.

But Paul's main point is that we're not to encourage other people to act contrary to their conscience. Because there's freedom, we're free to eat, and we're free not to eat. So we can use our freedom not to eat to avoid pressurising a brother or sister to act against their conscience (v 15). Forgoing your rights in this way is pleasing to God (v 18).

⌄ Apply

> ❷ *What freedoms have you forgone, or could you forgo, for the sake of others?*

What's really at stake
Re-read Romans 14:15 and 20

If we lead other Christians to act against their conscience, we may "destroy someone for whom Christ died" (v 15), and we may "destroy the work of God" (v 20). That's serious! If we encourage someone to ignore their conscience, we're switching off the inner warning system that God has given them to combat sin. Christ died to lead that person out of sin and condemnation, and now we're leading them back into sin and condemnation.

···· **TIME OUT** ·····························

There is a time for Christians to correct and disciple one another.

Read Galatians 6:1-6

> ❷ *What does Paul call us to do in these verses?*
> ❷ *What safeguards does he commend to ensure we do not overstep our role?*

⌃ Pray

Pray that you would be sensitive to the Christians you spend time with, and that you would get to know them so well, that you would know how to live to encourage and help them best.

Bible in a year: Isaiah 14-16 • Mark 4:21-41

The same attitude

Paul is still concerned with how we handle disagreement. In today's passage he gives us more reasons to bear with one another.

The power of Christ
Read Romans 15:1-2

❓ *What should we do, according to these verses?*
❓ *What should we not do?*

Often our sinful inclination is to put other people down to defend our rights. Paul calls us to do the exact opposite: not to please ourselves and instead to build others up.

The pattern of Christ
Read Romans 15:3-5

❓ *Who is our model, and what is our motive for putting others first?*

Despite being God's anointed King, Jesus did not please himself. Instead he sacrificed himself to build us up. He laid aside his rights to make us right with God.

···· TIME OUT ·························

In verse 3 Paul uses a quote from the Old Testament to exhort us to imitate Christ, God's ultimate King. In verse 4 he comments on this. Although the Scriptures were "written in the past", they were also "written to teach us". They speak in a personal way with contemporary relevance and power through the work of the Spirit.

The praise of Christ
Read Romans 15:6-12

❓ *What happens when we accept one another and build one another up instead of insisting on our rights or our opinions?*
❓ *What happens if we follow Christ's example and give ourselves to serve others?*

Instead of our churches having competing voices fighting for supremacy, we join our voices to sing of the supremacy of Christ.

The main division in the church in Rome was between Jews and Gentiles. So Paul uses Old Testament quotes to show that God's goal is to create a people from every nation united in his praise. Just as in a choir different voices combine to produce rich harmonies, so our differences combine in Christ to create something beautiful, to God's praise. Our corporate worship is a powerful celebration of our unity-in-diversity and a powerful sign of the reconciling power of the cross.

🔺 Pray

Use the words of verse 13 to pray for people in your church whom you find difficult. And use these words to pray for the unity of your church.

Ambition

What's your ambition? To represent your country at the Olympics? To succeed in business or climb the career ladder? To find love or have a family?

Paul tells us why he wrote to the Romans, and, in so doing, he reveals his ambition.

Read Romans 15:14 and 23-24

> ❓ *What is Paul ambitious for?*

Paul didn't write to sort out some kind of problem in the church. So why did he write at all? Back in 1:9-13 Paul says he plans to visit the church in Rome. But this is not to be a sightseeing trip. Instead, he wants to preach the gospel among them (1:14-15). But Paul's goal is bigger even than that: Paul wants to make Rome a stepping-stone for a new mission to Spain (15:24).

In this passage Paul talks about his duty and ambition. In one sense it's very personal. But he also wants the church in Rome to share this duty and this ambition. He wants every Christian to feel this missionary passion to take the gospel to the ends of the earth.

Our gospel duty
Read Romans 15:15-16

Paul describes proclaiming the gospel as a "priestly duty". It's the image of a priest going into the temple to offer a sacrifice. Christ has made atonement through his sacrifice once for all. So for Christians what priests and sacrifices mean has been transformed:

- The priest is every Christian.
- The temple is the presence of God.
- The offerings are new Christians.

Read Romans 15:17

> ❓ *How does Paul feel about this new kind of priestly service?*

Our gospel ambition
Read Romans 15:18-22

Paul's ambition is to preach Christ in new places. This passion has borne remarkable fruit all around the Mediterranean. But then Paul says that this is actually "what Christ has accomplished through me ... through the power of the Spirit of God". That's because this ambition is Christ's own ambition for his people.

✔ Apply

> ❓ *In what ways are you fulfilling your duty to proclaim the gospel?*
> ❓ *What are you doing to support the proclamation of the gospel in new places?*
> ❓ *How are you doing at proclaiming the gospel where you live?*

The struggle to reconcile

Paul's big plan is to proclaim Christ in Spain. But first he's going to make a massive detour. Why?

Via Jerusalem...

Read Romans 15:23-29

> ❷ *Can you work out Paul's travel plans?*
> ❷ *Can you work out the thinking behind this enormous detour?*

Paul really wants to come to Rome and he really, really wants to go Spain. But he's about to head in the opposite direction. That's because he's made a collection among some of the Gentile churches for the needy Jewish Christians in Jerusalem. He's about to go to Jerusalem to deliver this money. Only then will he go to Spain via Rome.

... with love

Read Romans 15:30-33

> ❷ *What do you think lies behind Paul's odd prayer requests here?*

Paul is heading to Jerusalem with a big gift for the church. He prays for safety from unbelievers. That's understandable. In fact, we discover in Acts 21 – 23 that Paul ended up being arrested in Jerusalem and coming to Rome in chains. But Paul also prays that the church will receive his gift favourably. And that is odd—because we don't normally worry about whether needy people will accept a gift. What's going on?

Paul has preached the gospel to the Gentiles. He's said that Jesus is not just the Jewish Messiah but the Saviour of the world. He's also said that Gentile converts don't need to become Jewish and be circumcised—faith in Christ is all they need because Christ has done everything needed. This has been what the letter to the Romans has been all about.

But not everyone agrees. What Paul calls "my struggle" is his battle to get Jewish Christians to accept Gentile converts (Romans 15:30). So Paul has collected money from Gentile churches for the Jewish church to bring them together. It is not a foregone conclusion that this gift will be well received. Paul hopes to come to Rome "with joy", but he might end up coming in sorrow (v 32).

Paul's prayer is that the collection will be a sign of gospel unity. Paul's fear is that it will become a sign of disunity.

✔ Apply

Paul has a strong commitment to gospel unity. He's literally going out of his way to be reconciled to other Christians.

> ❷ *What might this mean for you personally?*
> ❷ *How does your church express gospel unity with other churches, both locally and throughout the world?*

Pray for those associations now.

It's all about mission

The Bible is all about mission: God's mission to bring salvation to the world through Christ and our mission to spread that good news to all nations.

Read Romans 16:1-16 and 21-23

❓ *What strikes you about this list of people?*

❓ *What have they done or what are they doing?*

❓ *Are there any with points of connection with your life?*

The names suggest a range of ethnic backgrounds. There's also a mix of men and women. As the "director of public works", Erastus would have been a high-ranking citizen (v 23), while Phoebe was in a position to be a "benefactor" (v 2). As tentmakers (Acts 18:1-3), Priscilla and Aquila had a lower status, while others had names common among slaves. But all these people are brought together by the gospel and a shared desire to serve Christ. They have given money, taken risks, opened homes, been imprisoned, remained faithful, and worked hard because they share Paul's passion to proclaim Christ.

Read Romans 16:17-20

Not everyone who calls themselves "Christian" shares this passion for Christ. Despite all that Paul has said about the importance of unity in chapters 14 – 15, he wants us to watch out for false teachers.

Read Romans 16:25-27

The prayer at the end of Romans is full of echoes of its beginning. In 1:1-5 Paul says he is set apart for the *gospel* of God, which is regarding his Son ... *Jesus Christ* our Lord,

who was foretold through his *prophets* in the Holy Scriptures (literally "*writings*"), to be made known to all the Gentiles (or "*nations*"), so that they could experience *the obedience that comes from faith.*

We find the same big ideas at the end of the letter. Romans is about calling the nations to faith by proclaiming the gospel of Jesus Christ. This mission was promised in "the prophetic writings". The Christian life is all about mission because the Bible is all about mission. Mission is not just Paul's personal version of Christianity or a specialist interest—it's central to the Bible story. The stories of Abraham, Moses, David and the prophets come to their climax in your church as people from all nations come to the obedience of faith.

Apply

❓ *What you have learnt from reading Romans that you want to put it into practice? Try to write down three very specific things.*

Pray

What you have learnt from reading Romans that you want to turn into praise?

Finish your prayers by saying (out loud if you can) the words of Romans 16:25-27 for yourself and your church.

Going straight

God loves justice, as today's proverbs show—and we are called to love justice too.

Say it as it is
Read Proverbs 24:23-25

❓ *How do you feel when you see injustice in the world?*

❓ *Today, one incentive for judges to be impartial is a high salary, so that they are not tempted by bribery. What other reasons for impartiality are there here?*

❓ *Is this proverb solely aimed at courtroom judges? Why or why not?*

We might not all have the right to convict the guilty in a court, but we must all seek to distinguish between guilty actions and the innocent—whether that's in our family relationships, at work or as we react to media stories. If we have a voice to call out guilt, we must be mindful not to call that which is wrong "right".

▼ Apply

❓ *When can you say or want to be told that a guilty action is fine: consider speeding and lying, for example?*

TIME OUT

Read Micah 6:8

In Jesus we can see that God does not ask of us what he was not prepared to do himself. The cross shows God to be utterly and completely *just*—in punishing sin; *merciful*—towards sinful humanity as he bore the punishment we deserved; and *faithful*—in his promise to reconcile sinful people with their holy God.

Be part of the cure
Read Proverbs 24:28-29

Verse 28 is an application of the ninth commandment, "You shall not give false testimony against your neighbour".

❓ *Can you picture a scenario like those given in verses 28-29?*

Verse 28 reminds us that we can be part of the problem or part of the cure. We have solid reasons in verses 23-25 why we should not do this—the end of the unrighteous is destruction. But this verse calls us to reflect on how we can be tempted to want others to see our neighbour as guilty, even if they are innocent.

❓ *What does verse 29 tell us not to do?*

This is not a call to allow violence or evil to go unpunished. Rather, it is a reminder to us that there is a difference between justice and a manipulative desire for revenge born out of the heat of our hurt.

▼ Apply

❓ *When might you be tempted to use a person's past failings to call them guilty and exact revenge?*

❓ *How can the forgiveness you received through Christ challenge you here?*

1 CHRONICLES: Back to the future

An introduction

The books of 1 and 2 Chronicles might seem strange at first sight. They cover much the same ground as the books of 1 and 2 Samuel and 1 and 2 Kings but from a completely different viewpoint.

1 Chronicles is taken up with many familiar stories about David, but there's something missing. There's no Bathsheba, no Uriah: none of the "bad stuff" we read about David in 2 Samuel. It's the same with Solomon. *What's going on?* Is this simply a "fake news" version of events that whitewashes the heroes of Israel's history? Let's rewind the clock to understand what's happening here.

In 587 BC the Babylonians had captured Jerusalem, destroyed the temple and forced the Jews into exile. Seventy years later the Babylonians were in turn smashed by the Persians, and some of the Jews returned to repopulate Jerusalem and rebuild the temple.

But things were not as they had been promised for the returned exiles, who had been longing for a return to the promised land. There was famine; there was an economic depression. There were attacks from enemies. The rebuilding of the temple had stalled. Life in Jerusalem was hard. And there was a growing credibility gap between what the prophets had promised and what the people were experiencing. The prophets had made grand claims:

- Isaiah 40:1-5 promised that all God's people—and many more besides—would be gathered back to Jerusalem. But in reality there were very few.

- Isaiah 9:6-7 painted a picture of God's enemies defeated and of a son of David who would reign over God's people in justice and peace. But the son of David was just a governor in a land ruled by foreigners.

- Ezekiel 36:33-36 said that the land would bloom like the Garden of Eden. But there were still famines in the land, and the people were having to scratch a living.

It was to speak into this situation that the chronicler took all the historical sources he had and wove a new pathway through the stories of Israel's past to give hope to this struggling nation for the future. The books of Samuel and Kings had shown the reason why God had driven unfaithful Israel into exile. Chronicles shows what had been truly wonderful about the past, and points to a bigger and better future—a future that exceeds the glories of the past.

This credibility gap remains for Jewish people today but finds its resolution in Christ, who fulfils all these promises and so many more. God will gather people from all nations into a kingdom ruled by King Jesus in the new creation.

So Chronicles is a thoroughly Christian book; and we read its pages through the lens of its ultimate fulfilment in Christ.

Hope for today

Getting our heads around what the chronicler is saying and why is a bit tricky. Read the introduction on the previous page to get a feel for what's in store and why.

Brace yourself. If you struggle with the genealogies of the Lord Jesus in Matthew 1 and Luke 3, you're going to struggle with the first nine chapters of this book. It is a genealogy on steroids.

Back to the future
Read 1 Chronicles 1:1 – 2:2

As you read this list of names, try to call to mind the important thing that each of them represents for the history of God's people.

❓ *Where does the list start, and why might that be important as the Chronicles begins?*
❓ *After broadening out with the sons of Shem, Ham and Japheth, it narrows down again (1:27-28). Can you work out the significance of this?*

The writer wants to connect his readers with the first man, Adam. In doing so, he connects us to God's call to Adam and the whole human race—to know God and to serve him; but also to Adam's sin and curse. We all share his physical DNA but also his "spiritual DNA". The view zooms out with Noah's sons to embrace the whole of humanity but then focuses in tight on the family of Abraham, because to him was given the promise of blessing—a blessing passed on to Isaac and then to Jacob (=Israel). And note that it is God who makes these choices, not the chronicler choosing his favourite stories. He is simply charting the path of God's blessing.

⌄ Apply

The people in this list mark out the plotline of God's plan of salvation. As such, it was a massive encouragement to the first readers of the Chronicles. We only see a brief window of history unfolding before our eyes—the times we are living through now. But step back and we see people just like ourselves. Heroic and frail. Winners and losers. Wealthy and poor. But none of them forgotten; and all of them a part of God's great plan.

You are truly connected
Read Galatians 3:6-9, 14

❓ *Who are Abraham's real children?*
❓ *How are you connected to Abraham?*
❓ *What is your inheritance?*

Do you sometimes feel insignificant in the big sweep of things? All we know about many of the people we have read about in these verses is their names. They lived ordinary lives filled with love and laughter and sorrow and tears. Maybe they ended their lives wondering, *What was all that about?* And yet each of them had a vital role to play in God's plan of salvation. Each of them was used by God, important to God, and remembered by God. What is true for them is doubly true for you as an adopted child of God.

Hoping for a king

The chronicler now focuses in on his key theme: God's chosen King (Messiah) and the royal line that flowed to David, and from him to the future.

Sons of Israel

Read 1 Chronicles 2:1-2

God re-named Jacob "Israel" after his encounter wrestling with the mysterious man who turned out the be the Lord: Genesis 32:22-32. Israel had twelve sons , who fathered the twelve tribes of Israel. The next eight chapters of 1 Chronicles will outline the descendants of each of these sons.

> ❷ *Flick ahead through these chapters, noting from the subheadings the relative space given to each tribe:*
> - *Which sons get the most space?*
> - *Why do you think that might be?*

David's line

Read 1 Chronicles 2:3-4

When David's son Solomon died, his son Rehoboam became king, but ten of the Israelite tribes rebelled against him. Only the tribes of Judah, Benjamin and the Levites (the special priestly tribe) stayed with the line of David in Jerusalem. After the exile, the ten northern tribes were extinguished from history. So most of the Jews reading this were from the tribes of Judah, Benjamin and Levi—which is why they get more space devoted to them. They also get key positions at the start, middle and end of the narrative.

Skim-read 1 Chronicles 2:5-55

> ❷ *What dark notes are struck in v 3 and 7?*

David's son

Read 1 Chronicles 3:1-24

Reuben was the eldest son of Israel, with Simeon and Levi next before Judah. The reason Judah gets most attention is because Judah's line brings us to David. Judah matters because David matters.

And David matters because God promised that a descendant of his would reign for ever (2 Samuel 7:12-16). If God's people were to have any future at all, then this future had to lie in a son of David. Their only hope was the restoration of the line of David, which would bring a reign in peace.

⌄ Apply

Although the chronicler focuses on the positive, he is not ignorant of the dark side of Israel's history. The exiles looked for a restoration to the land and a king. But this hope was only fulfilled in the birth of Jesus. Matthew lays out his genealogy from Abraham, through David, to Joseph. An angel visits Joseph and greets him: "Joseph son of David..." Jesus is the promised son of David—the one the chronicler was looking for. He is the one who "will save his people from their sins" (Matthew 1:21).

Praise God that his promises of a Saviour have been kept.

Hopeful prayer

Have you ever prayed for pain to go away—a headache, a stomach ache or a heartache perhaps. If so, you have prayed "the Prayer of Jabez"...

What's in a name?

Read 1 Chronicles 4:1-23

❓ *Who does this section focus on?*
❓ *What does the name Jabez mean (v 9)?*
❓ *What was his character?*

In this chapter the chronicler concludes his list of Judah's descendants He focuses on Perez because this is David's line. But it includes someone with the name "Pain"— not a particularly honourable name in such a kingly line.

Naming in the Bible is important. A child might be named either as a reference to their origins or by their looks and features. But names could also be prophetic in some kind of way. God renames the childless Abram (=exalted father) to Abraham (=father of many). It might have been considered cruel, except that God's purposes were fulfilled in Abraham, who is the father of faith of *all* who believe.

Jabez means "pain", not because he was a pain to others but because his mother had experienced a particularly difficult labour (v 9). To make this clear, the chronicler tells us that Jabez was actually more honourable than his brothers.

Praying for blessing

Re-read 1 Chronicles 4:9-10

❓ *What did he pray for specifically?*

❓ *Is there any hint as to why he prayed this?*

The prayer of Jabez has received a lot of attention and has been singled out as a prayer that will bring blessing to those who pray it regularly.

Jabez was part of a culture that put great store by the meaning of names—they could become self-fulfilling prophesies. The girl called "misery" could well grow up to be miserable. So the name Jabez was like a curse. And so he prays that God will turn his curse to blessing.

But the significance goes beyond that. The chronicler writes to people in God's promised land—a land drastically reduced in size and living under the threat of harm. The chronicler wants to encourage people to turn back to God in prayer (see 2 Chronicles 7:14). If they do, then God will hear them and restore them to blessing just as did with Jabez. Today, Christians are not promised a life free from pain: in fact, quite the opposite—see John 16:33. But this prayer is for us a pointer to the life to come when we inherit the new creation and live with God, where there will be no more crying or grief or pain (Revelation 21:1-4).

⌃ Pray

Thank God that in Christ, this prayer has been and will be answered in the new creation.

Losing hope

Does your family have a "name" and a reputation? Perhaps you are known for wealth, or musicality, or good humour or kindness—or for something not so great.

The chronicler has so far focused on Judah and the line of David. But he's not being exclusive. He is concerned with "all Israel"— it's one of his favourite phrases.

Simeon

Read 1 Chronicles 4:24-31

The land had been parcelled out to the twelve tribes after Joshua's conquest, supposedly in perpetuity. But different tribes fared differently: some growing, some shrinking—either through war, bad leadership or, as hinted at here, through a lack of fertility. Shimei's huge family is mentioned (v 27) because it was the exception to the rule. The tribe of Simeon was not numerous and seems to have been absorbed into Judah by the reign of David (v 31). They never played an important part in Israel's history.

Two and a half men

Read 1 Chronicles 5:1-26

> ❷ What had become of the tribe of Reuben and why?
> ❷ Where had they migrated to?
> ❷ Did Gad prosper? How?
> ❷ What happened to Manasseh and why?

Israel was basically the area between the River Jordan and the Mediterranean Sea. But two and a half tribes—Reuben, Gad and half of Manasseh—chose to settle on the eastern side of the River Jordan. Being on the other side of the river meant they were easily forgotten, as they were far away from where the main action was taking place and more prone to invasion and suppression by the powerful nations to the east and north.

Historically, they may have become unimportant, but not as far as God's promises and purposes are concerned. The restoration of God's kingdom could never be complete until "all Israel" has been gathered in.

☑ Apply

The chronicler is not just concerned about ethnic Israel. Read 2:34 and 55. Egyptians and Kenites had a place in God's kingdom. Paul picks up the same theme. See Romans 11:25-27, where he wrestles with the same promises. God will gather in all his people, and they will be from every race, nation and tribe on earth.

☒ Pray

The good news is not just for all Israel, but for all nations— including nations we think are unimportant or we easily forget.

Pray today for obscure and forgotten countries (anything ending in -stan would be a good start). Pray that the gospel would reach into the lives of people there.

Hope in the temple

Where should we worship God? For fractured Israel it was a problematic question. They had a tendency to set up their own holy places on hills, but this was wrong.

The only temple

The chronicler wants to underline that the temple is the *only* place where God is to be worshipped, and where sins can be forgiven through sacrifice. So he puts the tribe of Levi at the centre of his genealogy because the Levites served in the temple.

Read 1 Chronicles 6:1-81

❷ *Which branches of Levi's family does the genealogy focus on? Why, do you think?*
❷ *Why did they need land to be donated to them (v 64)?*

Verses 16 starts what seems to be a standard genealogy. Three sons of Levi are mentioned and then each of their descendants in turn. But before this the writer picks out the line of Kohath (v 2). The line of Kohath is the line of Aaron, the brother of Moses and the first high priest of Israel. From him came the long line of high priests who served in the Jerusalem temple.

The Levites had no territory of their own because the focus of their work was the temple.

---- TIME OUT ----------------------------

Read Deuteronomy 12:1-14

❷ *Why was Moses so strict about where people should worship God?*
❷ *What does worship involve (v 5, 6, 7)?*

The only atonement

Re-read 1 Chronicles 6:48-49

❷ *What special job did the sons of Aaron do in the temple?*
❷ *Why is that picked out as especially important, do you think?*

Atonement in the Bible is making sinful humans "at one" with God: that is, reconciling sinners, who deserve death, to God, who is both just and demands justice. The sacrifice is a substitute for ourselves. Previously God accepted the death of the animal in the place of sinners, who were then free to enjoy God's presence with joy. Atonement was at the heart of the life of God's people then, but those sacrifices were not effective in themselves; the New Testament reveals that they were merely placeholders for the sacrifice of God's Son on the cross—Jesus, the Lamb of God, who takes away the sin of the world. On the cross, Jesus was both the sacrifice *and* the high priest.

^ Pray

Today, as then, an atoning sacrifice leads to us standing forgiven in the presence of God, with joy in our hearts and a song on our lips (see v 31-32)

Express your praise to God now for the sacrifice of Christ for you by using the words of a hymn like "In Christ Alone".

Hopeful future

In these three chapters the chronicler gives his rundown of Israel's history, and it's full of contrasts between what God's people were and what they had now become.

Past glories
Read 1 Chronicles 7:1-12

❓ *What is the mood of these verses? What does the writer keep mentioning (see also 7:40; 8:40)?*

❓ *How would the first readers—a small group of dispirited people—have responded to this, do you think?*

Israel was once a nation of mighty warriors—the local superpower for the region during David's reign. But now Israel is a small province under Persian rule. The writer wants his readers to remember Israel's history—to remind them of what once was.

Read 1 Chronicles 7:25-27; 8:33-34

❓ *Who is mentioned in passing in these genealogies?*

❓ *Why might they have only been given passing mention?*

Present realities
Read 1 Chronicles 9:1-34

❓ *What sources did the chronicler use to compile this information?*

❓ *What impression do you get of the numbers of people involved?*

❓ *What aspect of the life of God's people does the writer want us to focus on?*

Only people from four tribes plus some Levites returned to Jerusalem after the exile. The others are lost from history. This once great nation has been reduced to a pitiful state.

❓ *Why has this happened (see 9:1)?*

The returned Jews were a long way from all God had promised, because they had been "unfaithful" to their ever-faithful God. There remained hope for a full restoration but it was far from complete. The chronicler wants his readers to look ahead with hope, but this requires them to first look back. This has been the point of the genealogies.

❓ *What link does he want them to make with the past (see v 22-23)?*

The future for God's people will be found in faithfulness to God like that of Samuel, and in leadership from the line of David. They must turn back to God, as they find atonement through the offerings in the temple.

⌄ Apply

The Christian life is lived by looking ahead and looking back. In the celebration of the Lord's Supper, we look back to Christ's final and full atonement, and look forward to our inheritance—not in a physical land but in a new heaven and a new earth.

⌃ Pray

Look back and look forward now with gratitude in your heart. And then ask for your life to be a beacon of hope today.

✔ *Bible in a year: Isaiah 41-42 • Mark 10:32-52*

Grotty garden

Today we read a powerful pen portrait of how laziness has devastating consequences.

Observant wanderings
Read Proverbs 24:30-31

❷ *What does the writer witness in verses 30 and 31?*

❷ *How is the owner of the field described in verse 30?*

❷ *What reasons does the owner of the field use to explain its neglect?*

The picture is painted of a person who is not merely slow to take action but someone who is fundamentally lazy. "Sluggard" is a word used throughout Proverbs to describe a person who not only lacks initiative (19:24),but who invents reasons not to work (22:13) and still thinks he or she is cleverer than everyone around them (26:16).

✔ Apply

❷ *How might these first two verses be written if modernised for today? Try and avoid a farming or gardening example!*

❷ *Are there any areas in your life where you are most likely to show characteristics of the sluggard?*

Missing out on riches
Read Proverbs 24:32-34

❷ *Why is this a good time for a lesson?*

❷ *How does this sluggard show laziness, procrastination and a lack of self-control?*

❷ *What are the consequences of this?*

Poverty is not condemned here; rather, it is the wilful foolishness that leads to poverty that is denounced. The writer wants to leave us with no excuse; the make-up of our world is such that laziness does not reap rewards.

✔ Apply

❷ *How can you apply this proverb to your work, your household chores, your money admin or your relationships?*

In addition to areas of life where we can see material reward, this proverb also shines light on our spiritual lives. Consider the danger of a little slumber in place of getting up in time to spend quality time in God's Word. Or a little folding of the hands in front of the TV instead of going to the Bible study or prayer meeting. God's word is described as "more precious than gold" (Psalm 19:10). What riches we miss out on when we convince ourselves that our time would be better spent on some enjoyable but far less profitable pursuit.

❷ *What might the dangers be of overwork?*

▲ Pray

Pray that you would be someone who takes work (and rest) seriously.

And pray that you would be a "gospel grafter" in the soil of your own life and in the lives of others.

Hope disappointed

Well done for surviving the last nine chapters! But now the writer changes gear. So far, he has covered hundreds of years of Israel's history; now he slows down for the detail.

Much of what the chronicler writes is in praise of a "golden age" of Israel's history, which he paints in glowing colours. But David was not the first king of Israel…

Saul's life

Read 1 Chronicles 10:1-12

❷ *What aspect of King Saul's life does the writer focus on?*
❷ *Why do you think that is?*
❷ *Scan through 1 Samuel 8 – 31, looking at the subheadings in your Bible to remind yourself of the details of Saul's life. Why do you think all of this is left out of Chronicles?*

This chapter is almost word for word the same as 1 Samuel 31. It is clear that the books of Samuel and Kings were the chronicler's main historical sources. The big difference is that 1 Chronicles 10 is all the chronicler devotes to Saul, whereas 1 Samuel spends 23 chapters on him. What matters to the chronicler is revealed in what he adds to the account—1 Chronicles 10:13-14.

Saul's tragedy

Read 1 Chronicles 10:13-14

❷ *What lessons are we supposed to take from this sad tale (v 13-14)?*
❷ *Why is this particularly relevant to the first readers (see 9:1)?*

Saul was unfaithful to the Lord. And unfaithfulness was how the chronicler described the sin of Israel that had led to the exile. He keeps highlighting the link between unfaithfulness and judgment. This is both a warning and a hope. The chronicler warns us not to be unfaithful to God, for faithlessness leads to judgment in this life or the next. But the chronicler is also saying that turning back to God in faith leads to hope. And that is underlined by the last verse (10:14). Instead of a king that *broke* faith, we are introduced to a king who *kept* faith.

▾ Apply

One of Saul's sins was to seek guidance from a medium—the witch of Endor—instead of seeking guidance from the Lord (see 1 Samuel 28). You might not participate in such obvious occult activities, but Saul was just doing what everyone else did.

❷ *Are there ways in which you live by the wisdom of the world instead of the wisdom of God?*

▴ Pray

We know all about frail human leaders—in business, in politics and, tragically, in our churches. But we can have confidence that we have a perfectly strong, wise and good leader in the Lord Jesus. Praise him now, as you pray for the flawed leaders that you know.

 Bible in a year: Isaiah 45-46 • Mark 11:19-33

Hope dawns

The writer has connected us with the past, and has shown how Israel's first king was deeply flawed. The stage is set for the arrival of the next king.

King crowned
Read 1 Chronicles 11:1-4

❓ *Why does the chronicler want to emphasise these verses?*

❓ *Verse 2 describes the kind of king that David was called to be. What do the two titles suggest about his status and his responsibilities?*

In Samuel's account, there are four chapters of negotiation and uncertainty before David is crowned—although it is unlikely that there was an actual crown that he wore at this stage (but see 20:2). The chronicler leaves out all that. He goes straight to the point when the people acclaim David as king.

The narrative emphasises that David was accepted by "all Israel"—that he was king of a united nation rather than a coalition of fractious and independent tribes. He also deliberately makes the connection with the prophecy of Samuel, and with God himself. A covenant is made before the LORD (11:3). This is God's people united together under God's chosen king. The obvious point is that what happened once can happen again. There is a king coming—God's chosen King ("Christ" or "Messiah")—under whom we will be united and blessed by God.

Apply

Christians are those who acknowledge David's son, Jesus, as their King. We enter a new covenant with God through the blood of Christ. We dedicate our lives to his service and strive to be united with all of his people.

❓ *In what areas of your life do you struggle to live in submission to Jesus as King?*

Talk to him now about this, as you acknowledge him as the loving, caring Shepherd King over your life.

Apply

Is there a Christian you have fallen out with or find difficult to get on with? Your common allegiance to King Jesus is more significant than your differences. What could you do to restore your unity in Christ?

Capital chosen
Read 1 Chronicles 11:4-8

God had told his people to drive the Jebusites out of the land (see Deuteronomy 7:1), but they had never succeeded until David took command. From this moment on Jerusalem took on a special significance for God's people. It was the place where God was *present* with his people, for this was where the temple was built. It was also the place where God *reigned* over his people, for this was the seat of the kings of David's line.

TIME OUT

Read Revelation 21:1-4 and 22-24 to discover what Jerusalem ultimately points to.

Bible in a year: Isaiah 47-49 • Mark 12:1-27

Hope gives strength

We're familiar with the trope of a diverse but united band of heroes who join in battle to a common end: the Avengers, Charlie's Angels or Dumbledore's army.

Mighty God
Read 1 Chronicles 11:9-25

❓ How does verse 10 present the unity of purpose in Israel under David?

❓ Which deed of heroism do you most admire or aspire to in these verses? Why?

❓ Although the focus is on David's mighty men, who is the real hero (v 9)?

These stories of bravery, loyalty and heroism are thrilling portraits of courage and devotion to the king. But in all the stories of adventure we must not miss verse 9. David was powerful because "the LORD Almighty was with him". We may never again have clear and strong leaders like Jashobeam, Eleazar, "the Three", Abishai, Benaiah or "the Thirty", but the Lord Almighty is with us still. It is his blessing and purpose which mean that the kingdom of his Son will live and grow for ever.

☑ Apply

Being a follower of the King will require you to have courage. At some point you may face overwhelming odds, either numerically, or from a "giant"—someone with power and privilege. There may be moments when you are called to stand your ground and face whatever hostility comes at you, not with the world's weapons of violence, mockery or threats but with the quiet confidence that comes from knowing that God is with us.

United army
Read 1 Chronicles 12:38-40

❓ What is striking about the summary of the support that David receives from the people?

❓ What is the mood of the people living under David's reign?

The rest of chapter 12 continues the list of warriors who came to David's side at different times in his life. It emphasises again and again the support that David received from "all Israel", and how the differing qualities of the tribes fed into making his army invincible. And when God's people unite in obedience to God's King the result is "joy" (v 40).

Potential threat
Read 1 Chronicles 12:16-18

The loyalty of the Benjamites is in doubt because Benjamin was Saul's tribe. It is a tense moment, but the Benjamites provide a model response to God's king (v 18). They recognise who David is and submit to him.

☒ Pray

Thank God for the grace he has given you to recognise Jesus as King. And pray that he would give his amazing grace to others known to you.

Bible in a year: Isaiah 50-52 • Mark 12:28-44

The ark of hope

Since Sinai, God's wandering people had carried the tabernacle and the ark of the covenant with them. But now it was time for it to come to rest in Jerusalem.

Joint decision

Read 1 Chronicles 13:1-4

❷ *What is unusual about the way King David made his decision?*
❷ *What contrast is made with Saul's leadership?*
❷ *How does this show David to be a "shepherd king"?*

We are used to referendums and elections, but democracy was rare in the ancient world. The king and the people are seen to be completely at one as David suggests a course of action that all the people agree with. "The whole assembly of Israel" is involved in the decision. David does not abandon his leadership role but brings the flock along with him.

God's presence

Read 1 Chronicles 13:5-8

The ark was a chest covered with gold containing the tablets of stone with the ten commandments, a sample of manna and Aaron's rod. On top was a golden lid (atonement cover or "mercy seat") with carved cherubim (angels) on either side. It's not that God was shut inside the box, but the ark represented the presence of God with his people. It is sometimes described as "God's footstool", where heaven touches earth.

❷ *What aspects of God's nature are underlined in the description here?*

❷ *Why are the people so joyful?*

The journey of the ark begins with celebrations because the people are reaffirming the presence of God among his people. When the ark gets to David's new capital, God will once again be at the centre of things.

But then it all goes horribly wrong...

Curses and blessings

Read 1 Chronicles 13:9-14

❷ *What happens and why?*
❷ *Do you feel sorry for Uzzah? Why?*
❷ *How does the end of the story help us to see further into God's character?*

As far as we can tell, Uzzah had the best of intentions. The cart wobbled, and he instinctively tried to steady the ark. But the Bible says that the fault lay with him. The ark should have been carried on poles by the Levites, not placed on a cart (see 15:13-15). Uzzah should not have had to steady it. The problem was that the people didn't enquire of God. They didn't move the ark in the correct way. They were seeking to please God, but they didn't know God's will.

⌄ Apply

We must worship God with reverence and awe because he is holy. We can only approach God with confidence when we do it in the way he requires—through Christ.

King of hope

Think of this chapter like a "greatest hits" album. All the well-known tunes that get you smiling and singing along. None of the dodgy "B-side flops" that are best forgotten.

Great king

Read 1 Chronicles 14:1-17

❷ *What aspects of David's triumphant kingship are recounted?*
❷ *What is the secret of his success (v 10, 14, 16)?*
❷ *How are each of these elements in direct contrast to Saul's kingship?*

The contrast between Saul and David could not be greater. For David there is material wealth, many children, victory in battle and worldwide fame. For Saul there was defeat, with no son to succeed him, and his defeat was proclaimed to all the nations (10:9) with all the glory going to the Philistine gods (see 10:10).

⌄ Apply

It would be easy to apply this to us—saying here that we put ourselves in dreadful peril if we live in disobedience to God. That may be true, but the primary application must first be to see how this points to the faithful victory of the Lord Jesus. His faithfulness to his Father has led to his name being the greatest in all the earth—and he is delighted to share his honour and wealth with those he has gathered into his kingdom—you and me.

Great God

Re-read 1 Chronicles 14:10, 14, 16

❷ *How does God work to make his shepherd king great?*
❷ *How is this a contrast with Saul?*
❷ *How does this chapter make up for the problem in the last chapter? (It's subtle, but the clue is in the name of the place at the end of verse 11.)*

David is not the only person at work in this chapter. God is at work making David great. David both seeks and obeys the Lord in his military strategy, whereas Saul had disobeyed God and consulted a witch.

When David seeks God, God answers and directs the battles (v 10, 14). It is God who leads the attack on the Philistines (v 11, 15) and overcomes their gods (v 12). The God who "broke out" against Uzzah at Perez Uzzah (= "outbreak against Uzzah") in 13:11 now "breaks out" against Israel's enemies at Baal Perazim (= "the Lord who breaks out"). Behind David's greatness is the great and holy God.

Great commission

Re-read 1 Chronicles 14:2, 17

❷ *How do these verses point forward to the great commission of the church?*

It is our privilege to be part of this great task—the task of making Jesus famous among the nations

❷ *What will you do to make Jesus famous today?*

The God of hope

"If it's worth doing, it's worth doing properly." David appears to have learned his lesson about taking God's instructions seriously.

Faithful preparation

Read 1 Chronicles 15:1-17

> ❷ *How do these verses show that David has learned from the mistakes of chapter 13?*
> ❷ *How do you think the Levites felt as they obeyed the instructions and went to pick up the ark of the covenant?*

Everything is done properly this time with the Levites taking charge. David has learned the lesson of Uzzah—his abortive attempt to bring back the ark to Jerusalem. This time he is at pains to do everything correctly. You can be certain that the Levites took great pains to follow the letter of the law. They knew their lives depended on it!

Joyful execution

Read 1 Chronicles 15:15-16, 25-29

The moving of the ark is accompanied by a great celebration.

> ❷ *Why is there so much focus on their singing and music, do you think?*
> ❷ *How does verse 29 serve to underline David's faithfulness to God?*

Song of hope

Read 1 Chronicles 16:8-36

> ❷ *How should the people respond to the arrival of the ark in Jerusalem? What commands are given?*

❷ *What aspects of God's character are emphasised in this song?*

David's song begins by inviting people to "seek the Lord". Because the ark symbolised God's presence, people could in some way consult God through it (see 13:3). Seeking God is a way of saying that in all our decisions, we should place God's will and purposes above everything else, because...

... the Lord is "our God" (16:14). He remembered his covenant. He promised to give Abraham the land and he did so (v 16-18). He promised descendants beyond number and he made Israel a vast nation free from oppression (v 19-22). But his purposes do not end in a cosy mutual admiration society because...

... our God is the God of "all the earth ... the nations ... all peoples" (v 23-24). All other gods are mere idols, for only the Lord is the Creator (v 25-26). All the earth is invited to worship God (v 27-29) and submit to his good reign (v 30-33). This song celebrates the high point of Israel's life. But the chronicler writes at a time when Israel is tiny and ruled by others. Verse 35 becomes a prayer for the restoration of the rule of God's king. It is a prayer fulfilled in Jesus and is being fulfilled in the mission of the church.

Pray

Pray that you would contribute to that mission today.

Exalting yourself

Have you ever thought to yourself, "That person thinks highly of themselves"? What we mean is that such a person is lacking in humility.

Exalt yourself
Read Proverbs 25:6

❓ *What are the two instructions here?*
❓ *What sort of assumptions would a person have to make to show off in front of the king?*

To "exalt yourself" is another way of saying "show off". To "claim a place" is a type of self-promotion. And it comes as second nature to many of us.

"Don't they know who I am?" "I have a right to status because of my job, my achievements, my position." "I have important things to say." "I need to be heard." "What I have to say is more important than the opinions of others."

This proverb warns against a style of self-promotion that lacks humility before our leaders. And it can also be exhausting for others... Our friends or colleagues not able to get a word in because we consider our story worthier of airtime. The person we work with or in our church who goes unrecognised for their contribution because we quickly take the credit. Using the excuse of being self-assertive to advance ourselves at work at the expense of others.

⌄ Apply

❓ *When might you be tempted to exalt yourself in front of people:*
- *in the home?*
- *at work?*
- *in the church?*

Waiting for the call
Read Proverbs 25:7a

Imagine you are at a wedding and it's time for the photos. The photographer tells everyone to gather round the bride and groom. One person wants very much to be in the shot and to be seen as close to the happy couple, and so pushes his way to the front. How humiliating when she is told that is not where she should stand. She is told that she should move away to make way for the mother of the bride or the best man. In the words of Proverbs 18:12, "Humility comes before honour."

···· TIME OUT ····

Our confidence to stand in God's presence and call God our Father is not because of our goodness, as if God is swayed by self-promotion. Rather, he elevates us into his family—a place of honour—as he calls us by his mercy.

⌄ Pray

Pray for a heart that wants to honour Jesus rather than ourselves. Pray for our humility that thinks of others before ourselves.

Hopeful plan

David is planning a major piece of building work, but it doesn't get beyond the blueprint stage before God intervenes…

David's plan
Read 1 Chronicles 17:1-2

- ❷ *What is good about David's plan?*
- ❷ *What are his motivations, do you think?*
- ❷ *What guidance confirms his idea?*

God's plan
Read 1 Chronicles 17:3-15

- ❷ *What rebukes are there in this word from God for both Nathan and David?*
- ❷ *What bigger promises is David given instead?*

God does not need a house to dwell in. He has managed well enough so far. God does not need David. It is not what David can do for God that matters. It is what God himself does that matters—that is how God works to bring honour to himself in the world. God rescued his people and gave them a home of their own. God made David's name great.

David wants to build a house for God. Instead God is going to build a house (= a dynasty) for David. One of David's sons (Solomon) will succeed him, and *he* will build the temple. But more than that: David's kingdom will last for ever. One of David's descendants will *always* be God's King on earth. The chronicler tells the story of David to encourage people to look for a new David. What *was* (under the reign of David) can be *again* (under the reign of a descendant of David).

TIME OUT
Read Acts 17:24-25

- ❷ *How is "house building for God" ultimately a doomed exercise?*
- ❷ *How can Christians continue to make this mistake today?*

▼ Apply

It's never wrong to have ambitions to build for God and his glory—to plant churches, to start ministries, to take initiatives in evangelism. But *never* fool yourself that it depends on you, or that, because it is honourably founded or if it is undertaken with the best advice possible, it will succeed. God is working to bring glory to himself and is pleased to use our energy, our efforts and even our weak and feeble prayers to grow the kingdom of his Son. Ultimately that means that it does not matter if they work or do not work, or if the direction changes in ways you had not thought of (and may not like). We can be confident that God's work is growing for ever.

▲ Pray

Think about the plans you have for yourself, your family, your church. Have you committed them to the Lord in a way which will make you happy if they succeed or not?

Talk them over now with the sovereign God, who holds you and the future in his hands.

Hopeful humility

Imagine what an issue pride must have been for the good-looking singer-songwriter and military genius, God's chosen one—David.

Pride is putting yourself in the centre, and it can take many forms. God has just made David the most important figure in the world. And he has promised that David's descendant will be the most important figure in history. He has promised to make David's name great (v 8). It is striking then that his response is...

A humble prayer
Read 1 Chronicles 17:16-22

❷ *What aspects of his personal history does David reflect upon?*
❷ *What aspects of Israel's history does he reflect upon?*
❷ *What are the answers to his questions?*
 • *Who am I (v 16)?*
 • *Who are we (v 21)?*
 • *Who is God?*

When David looks back on God's goodness (v 16), he sees how far he has come: from shepherd boy to king (v 7). And when David looks ahead to God's promises, he sees God's goodness stretching out across the generations for ever (v 17). And so he asks; David's humility is reinforced as he grasps two key facts about God:

• **The Lord alone is the sovereign King.** David's greatness is not the result of his goodness, strength or cunning. It is God's doing. The same is true of the nation. It was God who redeemed the nation through awesome wonders (v 21).

• **The Lord is gracious.** God's power on David's behalf is not a reward but a gift. God does not honour David because David is above other men. It is God's gracious acts that exalt both David and himself (v 17).

✔ Apply

These two beliefs—in God's sovereignty and grace—are foundational to healthy Christian belief and a healthy view of ourselves. They are also the beliefs that are most under attack in our lives.

❷ *Which of these do you struggle most to believe? Why do you think that is?*

A believing prayer
Read 1 Chronicles 17:23-27

❷ *What two things does David ask for?*
❷ *Do you find these requests odd? Why?*

David has learned the secret of praying for what God really wants. Such God-centred prayers will *always* be answered.

✔ Apply

❷ *Are your prayers full of the things that God wants—the salvation of others, God's honour in the world, love and unity among his people to name a few—or are they dominated by your own wants, needs and struggles?*

Talk to the Lord about your answer.

Hopeful victories

We lap up the wartime exploits of great heroes, or the desperate fights they were involved in. These chapters recount some significant victories of David and his army.

On a roll

Read 1 Chronicles 18:1-17

- ❓ *What overall picture of David's power does this chapter present?*
- ❓ *Why are the tributes and metals that David seizes mentioned (v 7-8, 11)?*
- ❓ *Whose victories are these (v 6, 13)?*

1 Chronicles 22:8 tells us that the reason David did not build the temple was that he spent his life in war. Chapters 18 – 20 record David's wars, but the emphasis is not on glorifying David, but on how they glorified God, as David wins peace for the land, and the breathing space from warfare and the resources to for his son to build the temple. The final verses of this chapter show an organised state where justice and the worship of God are prioritised.

⌃ Pray

The Bible urges us to pray for those who govern us, but this chapter also reminds us that peace, order and stability are precious gifts from God. Spend some time praying, not just for government leaders, but for the many civil servants whose work enables the flourishing of life in your community.

Total victory

Read 1 Chronicles 19:1 – 20:8

- ❓ *How does David deal with the humiliation of his ambassadors?*

- ❓ *What is Joab's tactic in the battle?*
- ❓ *What is troubling about chapter 20?*

The kingdom of Israel was a unique institution—both the spiritual people of God and a political nation. God's saving purposes and his reputation were on the line whenever Israel was attacked. But as well as being effective as a military leader, David was also compassionate on a personal level. And Joab delegated authority to trusted fellow soldiers. The result is a picture of harmony and effectiveness that beat the size, wealth and aggression of a terrifying enemy.

The story of the capture of Rabbah in chapter 20 is told without a single mention of Bathsheba, Uriah and David's adultery, lies, betrayal and murder. The chronicler is not in denial about David's faults but wants us to focus on his extraordinary achievements instead.

⌄ Apply

Christ reigns over the nations, and one day he will crush all those who oppose him. But the church no longer extends God's reign by political means. We extend Christ's reign by proclaiming the gospel. The most important victories we look to are the rescue of those under the dominion of darkness. There is much to lament about the failures of the church and individual Christians. Nonetheless, we must rejoice and take hope in the incredible spread of the gospel worldwide.

Hoping for mercy

Just when things were going brilliantly… disaster struck. How many times have you heard someone say that? How many times has that happened to you?

Pride comes…
Read 1 Chronicles 21:1-8

- ❓ Who lies behind what happens in this chapter (v 1)? How do you think he "incited" David?
- ❓ What objections does Joab raise?
- ❓ What do you think might be the reason why this is sinful?

David clearly sinned by ordering this census. Joab found it repulsive (v 6), and God found it evil (v 7). Quite *why* it was sinful is less clear. But Joab's answer in verse 3 suggests that David should have let God worry about his military strength. David had many mighty men, but the chronicler has repeatedly underlined that their success came from God David should have trusted in God's power—not in his military strength.

Mercy comes…
Read 1 Chronicles 21:9-15

- ❓ Why do you think God gives David a choice?
- ❓ What is David's response? Is his answer a good one, do you think?
- ❓ How is his choice vindicated?

David is given a choice of judgments. He chooses not to be punished by Israel's enemies but by God (through plague) because he is confident that God will exercise judgment with mercy. "His mercy is very great" (v 13). And his confidence in God's mercy is vindicated, as God in turn tells the angel to withdraw and spares Jerusalem.

Judgment comes…
Read 1 Chronicles 21:16-30

- ❓ What does David ask for (v 17)?
- ❓ What does he get instead (v 18)?
- ❓ How do his dealings with Araunah (ESV: Ornan) the Jebusite show his seriousness about this?

David understands that God is just and so there must be judgment. He must sacrifice an animal in the place of the people. Judgment must fall on the sacrifice so that mercy can fall on the people. But the sacrifice of animals is only a pointer to what is to come. Years later, the hand of God's judgment would fall on David's offspring (v 17) outside Jerusalem. On the cross of Christ, both God's judgment and mercy are satisfied.

☑ Apply

The readers of Chronicles had experienced the judgment of exile. The chronicler wants them to realise that there can be mercy through atonement if they turn to God in repentance, as David did. And we too can experience mercy instead of judgment through the atoning sacrifice of Jesus.

Confess your sin to God now and seek his mercy in Jesus' name. Give thanks that God's mercy and forgiveness are yours.

Hoping for the future

This story of David's census and God's mercy in 1 Chronicles 21 leads directly on to the theme of temple building. The two are closely related.

Preparing the way

Read 1 Chronicles 22:1-10, 17-19

❷ *Where was the temple to be built (v 1)?*
❷ *What does that signify, do you think?*
❷ *Why was David not allowed to build the temple (v 8)?*
❷ *What measures did he take to prepare for the temple's construction instead?*

The place of mercy—the threshing floor where the angel of the LORD stood and where God relented in his judgment—was to be the location of the temple and the altar, where Israel's sins were to be washed away by animal sacrifice. Later tradition identified the place also as Mount Moriah, where Abraham had built an altar to sacrifice his son Isaac—although this is uncertain. Mercy and judgment were at the heart of Israel's religion and Israel's God.

David was not allowed to build the temple but his role was to prepare the way. He also gathered an astonishing amount of wealth and resources. At today's prices, the value of the gold alone amounts to over $2 trillion. Iron and bronze are less valuable now but were at the time incredibly rare and costly.

Preparing the builder

Read 1 Chronicles 22:11-16

❷ *What principles does David try to instil in his son, so that he will see through the job of building the temple?*

⌄ Apply

In David's words to Solomon there are principles for us as we seek to work for the establishment of the kingdom of Christ in our lives, in our family and in our churches:

- **God will be with you (v 11, 16).** If it is truly God's work, then we will never do it alone by our own effort.

- **Obey God's word (v 12-13).** Success in God's work comes from obedience to God's word.

- **Be strong and courageous (v 13).** It's easy to be swayed by threats or complaints, so we need to be strong and courageous as we pursue gospel growth.

- **Now begin the work (v 16).** It's easy to put off starting something for God or changing deep-rooted behaviour. The intentions are there, but we never get round to action. So David ends with a call to get on with the job.

⌃ Pray

Go through the list and pray that you would follow this advice where God has called you to serve.

Building hope

Organisations and households regularly go through reorganisations in response to changing circumstances.

And now David, having organised the building materials and the precious metals for the adornment of the temple turns his eye on those who will serve in the temple.

✓ Apply

❓ *How are you serving in your church? Could you offer to help in some new way?*

Staffing decisions

Read 1 Chronicles 23:1-32

❓ *Scan your eyes over 1 Kings 1 – 2, where the transition from David to Solomon is a long drawn-out affair with some intriguing plot turns. So why is 1 Chronicles 23:1 so different?*

❓ *What is the reason for the reorganisation (v 25-26)?*

❓ *What different roles does David now commission among the Levites?*

The chronicler's concern is not *how* Solomon came to power but *why*—to build the temple (22:9-10). Previously, there was the large and demanding physical job of dismantling the tabernacle and the ark and moving them from place to place. But now the Levites' roles are diversified for serving in a temple that would be static and permanent. Notice that there is a specific investment in music—enough for 40 full orchestras! But also security and crowd control (gatekeepers), management (officials and judges) as well as a generic group who, on a rota, would serve the day-to-day requirements of temple life.

The main job

Re-read 1 Chronicles 23:30

❓ *What was the main thing the Levites were charged with doing?*

❓ *How might that easily be forgotten in the run of daily life?*

❓ *Why do you think the Temple mattered so much to David?*

The tabernacle was originally called "the tent of meeting". Similarly, the temple was the symbol and focus of God's presence with his people. This was where people could seek God and discover his will. It meant God was at the centre of their lives, guiding and protecting them. But it was also the place of sacrifice—where sins could be atoned for. Judgment was symbolically placed on the sacrificial animals so that they died in the place of the people. Justice was done, and sins were forgiven.

✓ Apply

In the Gospels, we discover that Jesus himself is the true temple. He is the place of meeting—see John 1:14. And he is the sacrifice—see Hebrews 9:24-28.

Praise and thank him morning and evening.

The best policy

Three proverbs today that encourage us to discern when to speak and when to be silent.

Don't complain in haste

Read Proverbs 25:7b-8

❓ *What is the instruction in verse 8?*
❓ *What might the writer mean by "hastily"?*

This is not forbidding the reporting of wrongdoing. Rather, it is calling for discernment about hasty, impulsive, snap-judgment accusations. When we read the word, "court", our mind's-eye might immediately jump to the law courts. However, there is also the court of popular opinion. Our audience can include social media, the neighbourhood, the church family.

❓ *What dangers of "trial by the court of popular opinion" have you seen or read about?*
❓ *Why might you be put you to shame?*

This proverb reminds us to always consider "what comes next". Emotion or impulse can draw us into an argument, only for us to be shown up as knowing a lot less about the subject than our opponent. Similarly, public accusation hastily brought can lead to a demand for evidence from us that we might not have, leading to our shame.

Words that hurt

Read Proverbs 25:9-10

The scenario is given of you taking a neighbour to court. Whether or not your neighbour is guilty, the warning here is that you can have a lasting "charge against you".

❓ *What do you think that might be?*

This "court" may, once again, be the court of popular opinion. Someone might have chosen to share information with you in confidence, but when we blurt it out to others, perhaps even when we "share it as a matter for prayer", we betray the trust given to us and damage their relationship with us.

Read Proverbs 25:18

❓ *How are weapons of war a powerful image of misused words here?*

Using lies against another person is like assaulting them with a deadly weapon.

In all three proverbs, honesty is the best policy. Whether knowing facts before speaking, keeping confidences or not giving false testimony, all three verses warn against the damage to relationships caused by speaking first and thinking later.

⌄ Apply

❓ *How can we guard against such hasty accusations?*
❓ *How will you react to social media gossip in the light of this verse?*

⌃ Pray

Commit your words and how you use them to the Lord.

Hoping to serve

David made extensive preparations for building the temple. But he also looked beyond its construction and made detailed plans for how it would be run.

Going on the rota

Skim-read 1 Chronicles 24 – 26

Most churches have rotas—lists of who's doing what and when. 1 Chronicles 24 – 27 is basically a series of rotas. First up are the priests. They were divided into groups ("ministry teams" we might say today), so that each team could be given a time when they would be responsible for serving in the temple (24:19).

❓ *What is good about rotas?*
❓ *What is potentially bad about them?*
❓ *How are these potential problems addressed in 25:6-7 and 26:8?*
❓ *The chronicler thinks it's important to recite a list of 500-year-old rotas to his first readers. Why, do you think?*

✔ Apply

Rotas keep things organised, and stop particularly keen or gifted people being overworked or overburdened. But they can also open the door to people who are ill qualified to "take their turn". Cue terrible-tasting tea, horrible feedback on the church sound system, and glum-looking unwelcoming people at the door. But although the rotas here were chosen by lot, people were also clearly selected for the skills they possessed. That's fortunate because being born into a family of musicians doesn't guarantee that you won't be tone deaf.

Organised to serve

The chronicler wants to show how it was done in the past so his readers can do it like that again. He wants to show us how God's people can be organised for service.

✔ Apply

Read 1 Peter 2:4-9

Peter says the church is now God's temple and Christians are priests offering "sacrifices" to God. The temple was the place of meeting—now the Christian church as it gathers is the place where God is present and the place where God meets with people to guide, challenge and bless them. The temple was the place of sacrifice—but now we point to the sacrifice of Jesus for us, and the forgiveness and new life that are to be found in him alone.

Read Romans 12:1-2; Hebrews 13:15-16

❓ *What are the sacrifices that Christians now offer to God?*
❓ *How do you need to organise your time for service?*
❓ *What do you think you might be particularly equipped to do in God's service? How could you test that gifting with your church leadership?*
❓ *Do you need to be on your church's rotas more?*

Hoping for wholeness

Life lived under God was not just about personal devotion to the Lord and correct and expressive public worship in the temple. It involved all of life…

We've got it covered

Read 1 Chronicles 27:1, 25-34

❓ *What aspects of community life are touched upon in these verses?*

❓ *Again, why do you think the chronicler is at pains to show this to his audience?*

Soldiers, stores, farmers, wine, olive, figs, cows, camels, donkeys, sheep—all human life is here. The chronicler would love to see the reign of King David again. He longs for the day when David's son will once again rule over God's people. He longs for the reign of King Jesus.

But the lordship of Jesus is not just a spiritual thing. It's not just about religious activities in a temple. All human life is under the reign of God's King. We don't just serve God by being on church rotas. We serve God at home, at work, in school and in our leisure. Our whole life is to be lived for God's glory.

Hoping for the promise

Read 1 Chronicles 27:16-24

❓ *We get a list of the army officers over the various tribes, but what's missing?*

❓ *Why might that be (v 23-24)?*

This takes us back to David's census of fighting men in chapter 21. We are reminded that Joab didn't complete the task because he knew it was evil in God's sight (21:6-7).

On the plus side for David, we are told he didn't count the men younger than twenty "because the Lord had promised to make Israel as numerous as the stars in the sky" (27:23). This is a reference to God's promise to Abraham that his descendants would be as numerous as the stars (see Genesis 15:5). Counting the men below twenty was a way of planning for the future. You could work out how many fighting men you would have in years to come. But Israel's future hopes did not rest on their possible military might, but on the certainty of God's promise.

☑ Apply

Think about the main spheres in which you live: the office or factory or classroom, the home, the gym, the pub, the coffee shop and your church. For each one ask yourself:

❓ *What does it mean for me to live under the lordship of Jesus there?*

❓ *More specifically, is there one thing I could start to do that would commend Christ to others there?*

⌃ Pray

"Whatever you do, work at it with all your heart, as working for the Lord, not for men, since you know that you will receive an inheritance from the Lord as a reward. It is the Lord Christ you are serving."

(Colossians 3:23-24)

Ask the Lord for strength to serve with joy.

Hopeful handover

In chapter 22 David announced his intention to hand over the kingdom to Solomon. In chapters 28 – 29 this event takes place.

Except that, actually, the focus is not so much on the handover of the *kingdom* as the handover of the task of *building the temple*.

A word for the people

Read 1 Chronicles 28:1-7

❷ *Who was gathered for this hand-over ceremony? Why is this important?*

❷ *What does David repeatedly underline in his speech? Why is this important?*

God's kingdom—then and now—is not built on human achievement, but on God's gracious choice. God chose Judah, then David's family, then David, and here he has chosen Solomon. "All Israel" are gathered to hear and devote themselves to God's chosen king. David calls the temple "a place of rest for the ark of the covenant of the LORD". In Deuteronomy God said the temple was not to be built until the people enjoyed rest from their enemies (see Deuteronomy 12:10- 11). That's why the temple couldn't be built in David's lifetime (1 Chronicles 28:3). God cannot enjoy rest until his people enjoy rest.

A word for the son

Read 1 Chronicles 28:8-21

❷ *What promises from God does he repeat, and what are the conditions of their fulfilment?*

David hands over the temple plans (v 11-19) with two exhortations to Solomon (v 8-10,

20-21) which are based on previous exhortations to leaders (see Deuteronomy 17:18-20 and Joshua 1:7-9). Leaders must follow God's word (1 Chronicles 28:8) and must be resolute in keeping it (v 10, 20), with confidence that God will be with them (v 20).

▼ Apply

❷ *If you are in a position of leadership in any way, which element of these exhortations do you most need to hear?*

Whether or not we are leaders, we are *all* gospel workers. Jesus is building his church, as we work at belonging, loving one another and sharing the task of preaching the gospel. It is possible to do God's work for our own glory. But "the LORD searches every heart and understands every desire" (v 9). And that means we must "serve him with wholehearted devotion and with a willing mind".

❷ *How hard are you working?*

---- **TIME OUT** ----------------------------------

God's work of creation is over, and so he rests (Genesis 2:1-3). But God's work of salvation is not over, and so he continues to work (see John 5:16-17). God's love for you is such that he will not rest until you enjoy peace. Only after Jesus had made peace for his people through his death did he sit down at God's right hand (see Hebrews 10:11-14).

Kingdom of hope

The dispirited people of God that the chronicler was writing for needed inspiration to open their hearts—and their wallets—and to work to restore the kingdom.

....

A generous king

Read 1 Chronicles 29:1-9

❓ *Why is this project worth backing (v 1)?*
❓ *Why must it be something that everyone is involved in together, do you think?*
❓ *Where does funding for the temple come from?*
❓ *What is significant about the way it is given (v 9)?*

The task of building the temple is great, says David, because it is more than a building project. Solomon is building something "for the Lord" (v 1). And he's calling for the people to get behind the project—and that begins with their wallets. Funding for the temple comes from three sources: official funds (v 2); a personal gift from David (v 3-5); and gifts from the leaders (v 6-8). The key thing is not simply the gift, but the giving. The people and the king rejoice to see the wholehearted devotion of their leaders.

⌃ Apply

Perhaps you regularly hear the words at church "God loves a cheerful giver". It can be easy for us to lose the habit of being a cheerful giver—especially when times are hard and there are so many other calls on our resources.

❓ *What is preventing you from being more joyful in your attitude towards giving?*

A generous God

Read 1 Chronicles 29:10-20

❓ *How does David encourage the people to be generous?*

David's song of praise has one theme: all that is good and great about the people and the king can in fact be attributed to God (v 11). His song is prompted by the generous offering of the people. Verse 14 is still heard in many churches today when the offering is taken. The people are only giving back to God what God has given to them. God is the source of "wealth and honour" (v 12).

❓ *How is this song a fitting summary of David's reign?*

A glorious kingdom

Read 1 Chronicles 29:21-30

David's final act is to attribute *everything* to God's grace and power. All the greatness, power, glory, majesty and splendour of his reign belong to God (v 11). But we miss the point if we see this as a model for funding building projects. The temple was fulfilled in Jesus (John 2:18-22) and his people (Ephesians 2:19-22). The lesson for us is to give ourselves freely and wholeheartedly in the service of Christ and his people.

Give thanks for the glories of Christ's reign and growing kingdom now, and the wonders of the new creation to come.

HEBREWS: Jesus is better

We all experience times when we just have our noses to the grindstone, following Jesus out of duty and obligation instead of delight in how wonderful he is.

At those times it is easy to look over at something else—some other person or situation or community or way of living—and think, "That looks better." If that feeling is familiar, then the letter of Hebrews is for you.

It was likely written in the early 60s AD, but no specific author is named. The audience appears to be primarily Jewish Christians who grew up in Judaism but have believed in Jesus. Yet they have hit a snag. For whatever reason—perhaps the pressure of persecution and opposition—they are thinking about going back to Judaism. The author's response can be summed up in one phrase: Jesus is better. He begins by showing that Christ is the superior revelation of God.

A speaking God

Read Hebrews 1:1-2a

The author breaks all of history down into two parts.

> ❷ Verse 1: When did God speak? To whom did he speak? How did he speak?
> ❷ Verse 2: When did God speak? To whom did he speak? How did he speak?
> ❷ How does this put you, as a New Testament believer, in a privileged position?

The author is getting ready to tell us that Jesus is the full, final revelation of God and that God's new way of speaking in the "last days" (before Jesus' return) is better than the old way (through the prophets to Israel).

That is not to say that the Old Testament is irrelevant or wrong. Rather, it is simply a story without a proper ending. Indeed, God ends the Old Testament story on a cliffhanger: he promises to send a Redeemer to save his people. But his people can only wait, wondering who that Redeemer might be. Finally, that cliffhanger is resolved in Jesus.

King, prophet, priest

Read Hebrews 1:2-3

> ❷ In what way is Jesus the ultimate...
> • King (ruler)(v 2)?
> • Prophet (revealer of God) (v 3a)?
> • Priest (Saviour from sin) (v 3b)?
> ❷ How is our appreciation of Jesus enhanced when we hold all three of his "offices" together?

☑ Apply

We have the honour and privilege of living in the age of Christ, through whom God has fully and finally spoken. We have seen God break into the world in the person of Jesus who rose from the dead to share his glory with the world. People were longing to see that for millennia. But we are living in the "last days," when it has finally happened.

> ❷ Do you normally think of yourself as privileged in this way? Why/why not?
> ❷ God has spoken through his Son. How should that affect the way that we live, and where we turn to listen?

 Bible in a year: Exodus 25-26 • 2 Thessalonians 3

Easily impressed

When my kids were little, they thought mac and cheese with chicken nuggets was the greatest meal of all time. It just showed there was a lot of food they hadn't experienced!

We're all like that when it comes to where we seek satisfaction and fulfillment in life.

❓ *What things of this world are people easily impressed by? What about you?*

The thing that the readers of Hebrews were impressed by was not job security or money or relationships; it was angels. It seems they had begun to honour and venerate them.

TIME OUT

Read Isaiah 6:1-7

❓ *What was impressive about the angels that Isaiah saw?*
❓ *Can you think of other occasions in the Bible when people's first response to seeing an angel is fear? How is that different to how we often think of angels?*

Angels are amazing, glorious creatures of God. Yet they pale in comparison to Jesus!

Better than angels
Read Hebrews 1:4-14

To prove Jesus' superiority to angels, the author gives us seven Old Testament passages.

❓ *What is Jesus' "name", and why is it superior to the angels' (v 4-5)?*

Jesus has always existed; there was never a time when he was not God's Son (John 1:1-2). So what's going on in Hebrews 1:5? In the Roman world, when sons came of age, they were formally bestowed with the family name, even though in one sense they had

always had it. Jesus "came of age" when he was resurrected and ascended into glory (Romans 1:4). That was his great inauguration. And no angel ever had this status as the heir of the universe, the very Son of God.

❓ *Look at Hebrews 1:6. Why does it not make sense to worship angels?*
❓ *How does the writer show that Jesus is...*
  • *the Ruler of the angels (v 7, 8-9, 13-14)?*
  • *the Creator of the angels (v 10-12)?*

The author's point can't be missed: *You're impressed by angels, are you? Tempted perhaps to worship them, are you? But do you realize how impressed angels are with Christ? They are absolutely blown away by his glory. They cower before this King. He even made them!*

▾ Apply

Instead of being easily pleased with angels, or with whatever fills that slot for us—sex, money, power, or anything else—we must look to the glory of Christ. He is the One who has a name above all other names, who is the only person worthy of worship, who rules all things and who is the One by whom all things were made. It is Christ alone who should captivate our hearts.

❓ *Are you too easily impressed with things other than Jesus? What are some of those things? Take a moment to compare them with Jesus, just as Hebrews 1 does with angels. Then worship him!*

Be reliable

Have you ever been promised something that never came? Have you ever felt the pain of being completely let down by someone? Then you will understand these verses.

Refreshingly reliable
Read Proverbs 25:13

> ❷ *What is the job described in verse 13?*
> ❷ *Who, in our workplace, home, churches, could be the "messenger" and "master"?*

This proverb describes a person sent out to accomplish something for another. It can apply to anyone sent to deliver a message, asked to accomplish something in the workplace, asked to serve in a particular way in church life, and to a Bible teacher who should faithfully deliver God's word.

> ❷ *How does this person's actions affect "the one who sends him"?*

☑ Apply

Our God is a promise-keeping God. How should this encourage us to take our cue from him and be refreshingly reliable.

Depressingly unreliable
Read Proverbs 25:14,19

> ❷ *Why should we be careful not to exhibit these behaviours? What is the effect of these behaviours on others?*

Can you think of examples of someone who has promised much only not to deliver, verse 14 (if you struggle think "politics"!). You may have experienced the hurt of someone you relied upon at a difficult time in your life turning out to be unreliable. These proverbs show how crushing unreliability can be to others. It is not only disappointing but, the powerful metaphors in verse 19 suggest it can both cause extreme, nagging pain and cripple our progress.

TIME OUT

Read Matthew 5:33-37

Jesus taught that when we say "Yes" or "No", this should be enough to guarantee it will happen. Christians should be considered to be utterly reliable people, with consistent dependability.

☑ Apply

At various times in our lives, people will rely on us in various ways: e.g. to honour our promise to pray for them; to turn up when we said we would be there; to honour that rota commitment in church, to pay back what we borrowed. Our actions will either be like a snow-cooled drink in the heat or like the rain cloud in the desert that never surrenders a drop.

☒ Pray

Pray that your "Yes" would be "Yes".

And pray that you would be known as reliable and that this would serve God's church and be a blessing to others.

Bible in a year: Exodus 29-30 • James 1

Don't drift

Have you ever been out on the ocean in a boat? If you turn the motor off, you don't stay in one spot. Without doing anything at all, you drift in the current.

It is the same in the Christian life. Drifting happens very easily and imperceptibly. Which brings us to the first of six warnings that punctuate the book of Hebrews...

Pay attention!
Read Hebrews 2:1-4

❓ *What must we do to avoid drifting away (v 1)?*

❓ *What are the consequences if we fail to heed this warning (v 2-3a)?*

❓ *Why can we be confident that "what we have heard" about salvation is true? What reasons are we given (v 3b-4)?*

Here is something that we rarely want to admit: there is a part of each of us that tends to be drawn to things other than Jesus. Many things can lead us to drift. It could be suffering, which derails our faith; or opposition, which makes us want to give up; or busyness, which distracts us from our spiritual life. It could be holding on to sin instead of repenting. These things can draw us away from God. Or it could be a culmination of little things.

To be clear, someone who is truly saved, who is truly a Christian, cannot ultimately lose their salvation—although they may have periods of disobedience or backsliding. However, we are given this warning to spur us on and to make us examine ourselves. If we reject the message of Jesus, we will be held accountable, just as God held his peo-ple accountable in the Old Testament (v 2; see Exodus 32:35; Leviticus 10:1-3)—and even more so.

❓ *These are sobering verses. But what good news can we also see here?*

One of the things that reassures us most in our faith is when we see the Spirit at work in God's people around us (see the end of Hebrews 2:4). It gives us confidence that the gospel message is true.

🔽 Apply

The message that we must not neglect is the "great ... salvation" of Jesus Christ. We need to wake up and make sure we are proactively listening to it, because it is clear, trustworthy, and reliable. But we are all too likely to drift away if we don't pay attention.

❓ *What are some steps you might need to take to keep yourself from drifting away and missing the message of salvation in Jesus?*

🔼 Pray

Praise God for the "great ... salvation" available to us in Christ!

Confess the things that might be causing you to drift away from Jesus at present.

Ask God to help you to pay attention to the gospel message and graciously keep you walking closely with him.

The perfect pioneer

In 2:1-4 the writer warned us not to neglect the message of salvation. Now, he begins to tell us more about that message—how God became a man to save human beings.

To do this, the author first shifts the focus to who we are as humans.

What is mankind?
Read Hebrews 2:5-8

❓ *What is unique about human beings among God's creations?*

❓ *Compare these verses with Genesis 1:26-28. What is the special purpose for which God has made us?*

❓ *What has gone wrong, and why (Hebrews 2:8)?*

Humans stand out in creation: we are greater than angels. One day we are going to rule the world (see also 1 Corinthians 6:3). God made human beings to be the guardians, protectors, and rulers of his world. He intended it that way for his glory and our blessing.

Yet instead of judging and ruling over creation, the first humans subjected themselves to a created being—Satan (a fallen angel)—and listened to him. The ultimate result was that God's design for the world was profoundly broken (Hebrews 2:8). Now we need someone to restore humanity to the glory God intended.

✔ Apply

❓ *Think about some of the people you will encounter every day. How should this reminder of the distinctive glory and*

dignity of every human being shape those interactions?

The perfect human
Read Hebrews 2:9-13

❓ *How did Jesus bring about our salvation (v 9)?*

❓ *What is the end result for us, his people (v 10, 11, 12-13)?*

Jesus is both God and man. And because Christ is the perfect human being, he can deliver us from the problem we have got ourselves in to. By becoming human, he was able to "taste death for everyone."

Verse 10 doesn't refer to the moral perfection of Jesus (since he was always sinless) but to his effectiveness as our representative. By suffering as a man, he became a more sympathetic, more appropriate, more fitting high priest for us. Here is where we see how our salvation depends as much on Jesus' humanity as it does on his divinity. If he was not really human, then he could not really represent us. And if he could not represent us, he could not save us.

Jesus died our death (v 9), gives us his holiness (v 11), and will lead us to glory. In Christ, God promises to make us into the kind of humanity he originally designed. This was always his plan. Praise him for it now!

Able to help

In a court of law, it is unwise to represent yourself. You need someone who knows the system and who can make your case effectively. The same is true in God's courtroom.

In ancient Israel there was someone whose job it was to represent Israel before God: the high priest. These next verses in Hebrews show us two aspects of Jesus' humanity that make him a better, more effective high priest for us.

1. Perfect sacrifice

Read Hebrews 2:14-16

❓ *Why did Jesus take on flesh and blood?*

The ancient priests offered sacrifices, but Jesus offered himself. This is like the lawyer who represents you in the lawcourt actually going to prison on your behalf. Why did Jesus do that? So that he might defeat death (v 14) by defeating sin.

⌄ Apply

❓ *Do you fear death? In what ways does that fear manifest itself?*

Being freed from the fear of death should radically change our lives! We spend so much time thinking about how long we are going to live and planning for the time we have left. But in Christ we live eternally. We need to get the fear of death off our shoulders and conduct our lives in the knowledge that we are going to live for ever.

2. Perfect intercessor

Read Hebrews 2:17-18

❓ *What do you think it means to say that Jesus is...*
- *a merciful high priest?*
- *a faithful high priest?*

❓ *Why is Jesus both of those things, according to these verses?*

Jesus lived the life of a human being. This is critical to understanding why he is such an effective high priest: because he can relate to you and me. Jesus experienced everything we experience (beginning v 17). His life was marked by intense suffering and temptation (v 18). No one could ever go to Jesus and say, "You don't understand my life". It's us who cannot understand how much *he* suffered in his life. He endured temptation without ever experiencing the reprieve of giving in.

If he endured all that faithfully, then he will also be *faithful* as a high priest: always there for you, always praying for you, always acting as your good representative before God. Suffering also made him a *merciful* high priest. Jesus is compassionate towards us because he knows what it is like to be in any difficult situation we might find ourselves in. So now he is "able to help" us (v 18).

⌃ Pray

What are some of the struggles and temptations you are facing today? Bring them before your merciful and faithful high priest, knowing that he understands and is able to help.

Fix your thoughts

Ever watched a high-wire act? What's their secret? They keep their eyes focused on the destination and never look down. It works that way in the Christian life too.

New identity

Read Hebrews 3:1

❷ *In what three ways does the writer describe us as Christians (start of verse 1)?*

A radical identity transformation has taken place for Christians. God regards us as holy, we have a new family, and we have a new citizenship. You belong with Jesus; he has called you to his country. That is who you are. Therefore, fix your eyes on him.

❷ *How does the writer describe Jesus (end of verse 1)? What does that mean for us, do you think?*

Better than Moses

If you were a first-century Jew it would be hard to find a figure who ranked higher in your mind than Moses. He led the Israelites out of Egypt in the exodus, delivered the law, and set up the whole system of temple worship. Yet Jesus is much more glorious than Moses, as the writer goes on to explain...

Read Hebrews 3:2-6

❷ *What do Moses and Jesus have in common (v 2)?*
❷ *Why is Jesus better than Moses?*
• *v 3*
• *v 5-6*
❷ *What else does verse 6 tell us about our identity as Christians?*

Although Moses and Jesus were both faithful, it is Jesus who is most worthy of honour. He is the builder of the house, not merely part of it (v 3-4). He is the Son of God, not merely a servant (v 5-6).

✔ Apply

Let me draw out a couple of implications.

First, notice that there is only one house. The author is not contrasting Moses' house with Jesus' house. It is all one house. There is a single people of God throughout all the history of the world.

Second, as followers of Jesus we are God's house together. He not only lives in individual Christians by the power of the Holy Spirit; we are all "being built together to become a dwelling in which God lives" (Ephesians 2:22). The Spirit of God lives in his corporate body, the church. That means it is vital to be committed to one another and linked together as his people.

❷ *What does it mean to you to know that you are in the same people of God as Moses? How should that idea shape the way that you read and think about the Old Testament?*
❷ *How does the image of God's people as God's house challenge our culture of individualism? In what specific ways does it need to correct your attitudes and actions?*

Warnings for wanderers

Yesterday we read that we are God's house, "if indeed we hold firmly to our confidence" (3:6). This cues up Hebrews' second major warning about falling away.

Hard-hearted

Read Hebrews 3:7-19

In Psalm 95, which is quoted here, God is warning the reader not to make the same mistake as that wilderness generation which failed to enter the promised land. The Israelites had been graciously delivered out of the land of Egypt and were heading for Canaan, a land described as flowing with milk and honey. But most never got there.

❓ *Why not?*
- *v 8-11*
- *v 16*
- *v 17*
- *v 18*
- *v 19*

⸱⸱⸱ **TIME OUT** ⸱⸱⸱⸱⸱⸱⸱⸱⸱⸱⸱⸱⸱⸱⸱⸱⸱⸱⸱⸱⸱⸱⸱⸱⸱⸱

The grumbling came to a head in Numbers 14. Spies had been sent into Canaan and had come back with scary descriptions of its powerful inhabitants. Read the story of their rebellion for yourself in **Numbers 14:1-38**.

❓ *What does the author tell us to do to avoid the same mistake (Hebrews 3:12-15)?*
❓ *What does that look like, do you think?*

Again, we should remember that to "fall away" (v 12) is not a reference to a genuine believer losing their salvation. Rather it is a reference to someone inside the covenant community who seems like a believer, but later proves to have an unbelieving heart.

✔ Apply

There are three things we should observe about this warning. First, the warning proves that having great spiritual privileges does not guarantee true, saving faith. Think of all the miracles that the Israelites had seen. And yet most still did not believe. When it comes to who is saved, God has a habit of overturning our expectations.

Second, this warning applies to everyone. Our temptation is to think to ourselves, "I don't need to listen to this warning because I believe in God". But, the Israelites could have said the same thing! We need to take the warnings seriously and urgently—while it is still "today"! We should be regularly exhorting one another to press on and not drift away (v 13). Accountability is a great ally in the war against apostasy. We all need it.

Third, a good start does not guarantee a good finish. Someone might start their Christian life with excitement and optimism, but the real test is whether a person demonstrates perseverance (v 14). Steadfastness is the test of the true believer.

❓ *What causes you to doubt, grumble, or complain in your relationship with God? In what areas are you at risk of becoming hard-hearted? Who could you talk to, so they can encourage you?*
❓ *What believer could you encourage today? Do it now! Pray for them and then call or message them.*

True rest awaits

Are you feeling tired? You're not the only one. A recent article in Forbes magazine found that nearly 40% of Americans sleep less than six hours a night.

With the sobering lesson of the wilderness generation still echoing in the background, our author then makes a remarkable statement in 4:1: "The promise of entering [God's] rest still stands". In other words, whatever rest God offered the Israelites is still available to the readers of Hebrews (then and now), since the ultimate rest God had in mind was not a physical plot of land. But the question is: how do we get that rest?

Read Hebrews 4:1-11

> ❷ *How does someone enter God's rest—both in the Old Testament and now (v 1-3a, v 6-7)?*
> ❷ *What kind of rest is the author talking about in verses 3b-5 and 9-10? How is that different from the rest that Joshua led the Israelites to (v 8)?*
> ❷ *What does the author exhort us to do in verse 11 to make sure we enter that rest?*

Ever since the creation week ended, God has enjoyed a perpetual, eternal Sabbath in heaven (v 3-4). This doesn't mean God is inactive—he is busy in all sorts of ways (John 5:17)—but he is still resting from his work of creation. And those who believe in Jesus get to join God in this eternal Sabbath rest.

On that day, our labours will finally come to an end (Hebrews 4:10). The "works" here are the trials and tribulations of our own journey in the "desert" on the way to the heavenly promised land. When we get to heaven, our journey will be over and we can finally rest.

Of course, as soon as we believe in Christ and the Spirit comes to dwell within us, we can enjoy a dimension of rest even in the present. Yet the overall thrust of the entire passage is forward looking (v 19). Our ultimate rest is still to come.

✓ Apply

> ❷ *In what ways are you feeling weary of life in the desert? How does this promise of Sabbath rest encourage you?*

The big point is hard to miss. Be serious about making sure you don't end up like the Israelites, dying in the desert and failing to enter God's rest. "Today" is the day of salvation. Don't put off examining your heart. The passage suggests one way to do that: Israel's lack of faith was evident in their disobedience (v 6). While we are not saved by our obedience—we are only saved by faith in Christ—our obedience can be a test of whether our faith is real. So, how's the fruit of obedience in your life today?

Hebrews 4:11 reminds us that effort, diligence, and perseverance are essential to the Christian life. We are not saved by our efforts, but by the grace of Christ—yet the Christian life still involves effort! It is not passive and detached but active and intentional. But one day, there will be no more striving, no more temptations, no more trials. There will be peace and rest for ever with Jesus (v 10). This is our great hope today.

Open and shut case

I think, therefore I speak. What a difference it would make in our world if the amazing gift of speech was more carefully used.

Right or wrong?

Read Proverbs 25:11

❷ *How does verse 11 describe a "rightly-given ruling"?*

❷ *How might well-chosen words be like jewellery?*

"Well here's what I think..." Have you ever heard this, or said it yourself? People seem very free to offer their opinion on anything. There are times when we want to give our verdict, or opinion. And yet, verse 11 reminds us that our opinions can be rightly or wrongly given.

❷ *When might our "ruling" be untimely?*

True but untimely

Read Proverbs 25:20

It matters when and where we speak. "A ruling rightly given" can be something people treasure. But these two proverbs encourage us to stop and assess the situation before we speak—even when we are confident that it is the truth that is coming out of our mouth. We can speak the truth at the wrong moment. We need to ask: *Are we in public, are we in private? Are they in the right frame of mind to hear what we will say? Is this the right moment to say this, or do they need my silent comfort and reassurance instead?*

Be careful of thinking you must speak because it is true; it may be true, but will your words be timely?

Careful correction

Read Proverbs 25:12

❷ *What is the purpose of a rebuke?*

❷ *What makes a wise rebuke?*

❷ *What does this rebuke mean for the person listening?*

No one likes being told off, but, as implausible as this might seem to the person on the receiving end of a rebuke, carefully chosen words of rebuke should be a thing of beauty—something you are happy to carry around with you, because you understand that they are extremely valuable.

Apply

If you have children, how considered are you when you need to rebuke them? Do you think about what you are going to say first in order to help them wear the message like an earring they are happy to adorn?

If you're a manager in the workplace, needing to call out a colleague's attitude or approach to their work, do you leave them with a stinging soliloquy or with careful, caring correction?

If you need to call out sin in a Christian friend, will your words be heard as unloving and self-righteous—or like fine gold to prize?

Pray that your timely words would build up and not tear down.

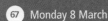

God's word in 3 words

If you had to choose three words to sum up how you think and feel about the Bible, what would they be?

Read Hebrews 4:12-13

At first glance, it may seem as though our author has suddenly changed topic. But these verses flow quite directly from the prior verses. In verse 11 we received yet another warning that we should obey God, lest we fall away like the Israelites. Here, the author explains why we should listen to God.

❓ *In what way do these verses show us that God's word is...*
- *personal?*
- *powerful?*
- *penetrating?*

❓ *Can you think of times when you have found that to be true in your own experience?*

God's word is "alive" (v 12)—that is, a living person is revealed in it. Since God's word is empowered by the Holy Spirit, when we encounter the word, we encounter God. It is through God's word that we meet him, learn from him, and have fellowship with him. In this way, the word is remarkably **personal**.

God's word is also "active"—the Greek is *energes*, which is where our English word "energy" comes from. The word of God is **powerful**. It doesn't just say things; it does things. It is busy working, changing, building, convicting, encouraging, exposing, rebuking, giving light and wisdom, carving out the path of our lives, and showing us the truth of God.

Third, God's word is designed to cut. Indeed, it is made for **penetrating** the hardest substance on the planet—not granite or diamonds but something even harder: the human heart. It exposes who we are. When you read the Bible and let it penetrate your heart, you will see things about yourself that you never saw before: your real intentions, motives, and character.

All that together makes one simple point. Is God's word trustworthy and should we rely on it and believe its promises? The answer is absolutely "Yes".

⌄ Apply

❓ *Since God's word is personal, what should your expectations and attitude be when you come to read it or hear it preached?*

❓ *Since God's word is powerful and penetrating, what implication should that have on how we seek to change and grow?*

⌃ Pray

Blessed Lord, who caused all holy Scriptures to be written for our learning: Grant us so to hear them, read, mark, learn, and inwardly digest them, that we may embrace and ever hold fast the blessed hope of everlasting life, which you have given us in our Saviour Jesus Christ; who lives and reigns with you and the Holy Spirit, one God, for ever and ever. Amen.

(The Book of Common Prayer)

A great high priest

In Hebrews 4:14 our author comes back to the theme of Christ as high priest. He is showing us that Jesus is better than the Old Testament high priests.

Why does this matter? Because all of us are in a perilous position as we stand before the holy court of God. We need somebody to speak for us, act for us, intercede for us, and represent us. Thankfully, we have someone!

Read Hebrews 4:14-16

❷ *What makes Jesus an effective intercessor between us and God? Think about:*
- *where he is (v 14).*
- *who he is (v 14).*
- *how he lived on earth (v 15).*

❷ *"Since we have a great high priest", what does the author encourage us to do (v 14, 16)?*

❷ *How are these three verses connected? Trace the line of argument.*

The high priest would enter the Most Holy Place in the temple once a year on the Day of Atonement and make a sacrifice for the people of God (Leviticus 16). But Jesus "ascended into heaven" (Hebrews 4:14)— the real heavenly temple itself. And he can intercede for us for ever because he is the eternal Son of God.

But what is amazing about Jesus is that he doesn't just act God-ward; he acts man-ward. He sympathizes with our "weaknesses" (v 15) and can relate to our temptations. He "has been tempted in every way just as we are—yet he did not sin" (v 15).

Jesus' perfection and purity are important because his righteous deeds are credited to our account. By your faith in Jesus, you are perfect in God's eyes because Christ's righteousness covers you and wraps around you. All of this hangs on the fact that Christ was sinless.

The result is that we can "approach God's throne of grace with confidence" (v 16). This is not the confidence that says, "I'll be fine before God because I'm a pretty good person". No, this is confidence not in yourself but in Christ and in his perfect representation. You can march right into the throne room of God, saying, "I am God's child. Jesus has saved me". We have amazing access to God by virtue of what Christ has done.

Apply

We have a deep human desire for sympathy. We often spend a lot of our time and energy trying to solicit compassion from others—displaying reasons why we deserve more attention. But if we have drunk deeply of the compassion available to us in Christ, we no longer have to find ways to get it from others. Go to Christ, who fully sympathises with your weaknesses, and then you can serve others by showing them the very sympathy and compassion that was shown to you.

❷ *What are you most challenged and encouraged by, from today's reading?*

❷ *How will it shape how you pray now, and how you live today?*

Perfect submission

In chapter 5 the writer to the Hebrews develops the theme of Christ's priesthood more fully—showing us why he is able to fully purify us from sin.

Read Hebrews 5:1-10

Old Testament high priests were selected "from among the people" (v 1).

- ❓ *Why was this a good thing (v 2)?*
- ❓ *What was the disadvantage (v 3)?*
- ❓ *Look at verses 7-10. What is similar between Jesus and the OT priests? What is different? Who is better, and why?*
- ❓ *What other similarity between Jesus and the OT priests does the author highlight in verses 4-6? How does this further emphasize Jesus' humility?*

To say Jesus "learned obedience" (v 8) is not to suggest he was ever disobedient. Rather, it emphasizes Jesus' experience as a human being who learned what it was like to obey God even in the midst of great suffering—an experience that allowed him, at a later point, to be "obedient to death—even death on a cross" (Philippians 2:8). His obedience made him our "perfect" high priest (Hebrews 5:9). Because he remained sinless, he could be a sacrifice on our behalf instead of having to pay for his own sins.

TIME OUT

The language in verse 7 likely refers to Jesus' cries to his Father in the Garden of Gethsemane. **Read Luke 22:39-44.**

- ❓ *How do we see Jesus' "reverent submission" in these verses?*
- ❓ *Did God hear his prayer? What was his answer?*

✔ Apply

Submission is not easy. It means willingly, humbly recognising the authority of another over you. Jesus' cries expressed his willingness to submit to whatever God had prepared for him—however difficult it would be. God heard his prayer, but he did not release him from suffering. God said no. And Jesus submitted to that, too. His obedience was radical.

When God tells you *no*, it is hard to submit. But Christ models for us submission to what might be the greatest "no" that anybody has ever received.

The school of suffering is not an easy one. But it can teach us, train us, and shape us like no other school, making us more effective ministers to others. We can, like Jesus, ask the Father to relieve us and comfort us. But whether the answer is yes or no, we must remain obedient to God. And—praise God—we can remember that we have a great high priest who is able to sympathise with our weaknesses.

- ❓ *How have you learned reverent submission from the school of suffering over the years?*
- ❓ *Is there some area of your life where it seems that God is saying "no" to you right now? What would Christlike submission in this area look like?*

Grow up

Imagine a grown adult who only drinks milk and has never moved on to solid food. If you met such a person you would think that something must be seriously wrong.

But that is exactly what our author says his readers are like, spiritually speaking. Here he starts off his third warning passage (5:11 – 6:12) by saying, *I'm worried about you...*

Spiritual toddlers

Read Hebrews 5:11-14

❓ *In what ways are the Hebrews like toddlers? What are the symptoms of being spiritually immature?*

❓ *Why aren't they growing (v 11)?*

❓ *What are the problems with remaining immature (v 12, 14)?*

The writer gives four characteristics of these spiritual toddlers: they don't listen very well (v 11); they are forgetful (v 12); they are unskilled (v 13, ESV—that is, they have not learned how to rightly understand the word of God); and they are undiscerning (v 14). That is actually a pretty good description of any toddler! The audience of this letter "ought to be teachers" by now (v 12). Instead they have become only takers in the church and not givers. They have become high-maintenance toddler Christians.

Have you ever seen a documentary of lions hunting wildebeest in the Serengeti? You'll notice that they always go for the babies first. It is the same in the Christian life. If you are not growing up in your faith, you are more susceptible to those who want to trick and deceive you and take you down wrong paths (v 14).

Elementary, my dear

Read Hebrews 6:1-3

❓ *What are the basic Christian doctrines that the author lists here, and what is their significance, do you think?*

By "move beyond" the writer doesn't mean leave them behind, but build on them; add to them. Elementary doctrines are very important. But there is so much more to learn! There is so much more growth possible. Don't be satisfied with milk when you could be enjoying a wonderful steak dinner.

⌄ Apply

Look over those four characteristics of spiritual toddlers and do a little spiritual assessment of your own Christian growth. Ask yourself: If I look back at myself five years ago, is there any difference now? Can I see God's work in me? Am I moving closer to God and not further from him? Am I serving those around me? Am I growing in the fruit of the Spirit (Galatians 5:22-23)? Am I helping others to learn the truth? Am I growing in my understanding of God?

Growth is not about earning God's affection. Like any good parent, God loves us endlessly already. Even if the toddler never really does grow up, it will not mean he or she is any less loved. But for our own good, he wants us to grow up and to mature.

A sober warning

Heb 6 v 11 - 12 Don't stagnate

Today we come to some of the most difficult verses in the entire book of Hebrews: the most controversial and debated, and perhaps most frightening. They concern apostasy.

An apostate is someone who once *seemed* to be a believer, but who later totally rejects Christ and leaves the church.

Impossible

Read Hebrews 6:4-8

❷ *In what ways did the people being described here look like true believers? What privileges did they enjoy (v 4-5)?*

❷ *Why does God take apostasy so seriously (v 6)?*

❷ *In what way is such a person just like land that soaks in rain but produces weeds (v 7-8)?*

Just like the Israelites we read about in Hebrews 3 – 4, it is possible to experience many blessings—to hear the truth, taste the Lord's Supper, participate in the local church and what the Spirit is doing through it, and weekly sit under the word of God— yet still say, "No, thank you. I don't believe it". That is what makes an apostate so culpable. These verses seem to describe a certain kind of rejection of God which leads to God giving a person over to their sin (see Romans 1:28; also Matthew 7:22 and 13:1-23).

However, there is hope. When we see someone leaving the covenant community, we don't know for certain that they are an apostate. Some people have periods of rebellion and resistance, and church discipline can bring them back in. It's the person who perseveres in their apostasy that proves they are a true apostate.

Pray

Do these verses make you fearful for particular people you know? Pray for them now, asking God to be merciful to them.

Signs of salvation

Read Hebrews 6:9-12

❷ *Why is the writer optimistic concerning the readers of Hebrews (v 9)? What signs of true faith does he see in them (v 10)?*

❷ *What does he encourage them to do in verses 11-12?*

Every true believer produces fruit. There may not be all the fruit we want there to be, but there is fruit—some willingness to labour for God, some affection for his name, and some love for his people. So the writer gives us a little nudge down the right path (v 11). The Christian life is a labour for the long haul—we need patience to finish the race (v 12).

Apply

❷ *When you look at the fruit in your life, where are you encouraged that God is at work? Where are you discouraged?*

❷ *What are some practical ways you can be "diligent" in faith?*

river
Life - on a conveyor belt:
can't stay still.

We have an anchor

In the Christian life, it can often feel like you are about to be pulled away by the currents—by things that make you doubt God. We need an anchor to hold us secure!

❷ *What doubts do you struggle with? Are there promises in the Bible that you question whether God will deliver on?*

God reassures us here in Hebrews 6 that we have great reasons to trust his promises. There are three strands in the anchor rope: God's oath, God's character, and God's Son.

Abraham our example
Read Hebrews 6:13-18

❷ *How does the story of Abraham help us to have confidence in God's promises (v 13-15)?*
❷ *Why did God swear an oath "by himself", do you think (v 13, 16-17)?*
❷ *What things about God are we reminded of in these verses (v 17-18)? How does this help us to trust his promises?*

God did not need to swear an oath. His promises are always true. But he swore an oath to Abraham in order to help him. God's oath is an act of grace—not because his word is in doubt but because *we* are in doubt. He recognizes how weak we are. Yet we can rely on God's character (v 17-18): his purposes do not change and he does not lie.

···· TIME OUT ·····································

Read some of God's promises in Scripture, and rejoice that you can be confident that God will deliver: **Luke 12:22-31; Hebrews 13:5; Ephesians 1:7 and 3:16; Colossians 3:4.**

Christ our anchor

The "two unchangeable things" (God's oath and character) are reason enough to have hope. But there's a third strand to the rope...
Read Hebrews 6:19-20

❷ *Where is Jesus now? How does that help with our doubts?*

Why should you be confident that God is going to keep his promises? Because of what Jesus has done. That is the essence of this anchor of the soul. The Most Holy Place in the temple, where God's presence dwelt, was blocked off by a huge curtain. It sent a clear message: God is holy and as a sinful person you cannot have access to him. But Jesus has gone behind the curtain, so to speak—into the heavenly Most Holy Place as "forerunner ... on our behalf" (v 20).

Anchors typically go down. But this anchor of the soul goes up. It is an anchor in heaven for you to hold on to. If you are in Christ, you have a place there that will never be taken away. This is the hope set before us, to which we must hold fast (v 18). (Note: we'll think more about Melchizedek, mentioned in verse 20, over the next two studies.)

⌄ Apply

❷ *How does what you've read today reassure you about the doubts you thought about earlier?*

Ever the diplomat

Try googling "managing your manager", and you'll find lots of books and advice on how to control your boss. They may very well be excellent books, but start here first!

Persuading

Read Proverbs 25:15

> ❓ *Who, in your life, could fall into the '"ruler" role?*

Boss, team leader, teacher, house-group leader, church minister? While these people may not be "rulers" in the strict sense of the word, they may have some sort of oversight role. This proverb is realistic that sometimes we might be in the right, while the "ruler" may need correcting.

> ❓ *What is the temperament that is encouraged in this proverb?*
> ❓ *What benefit does this proverb say could follow?*

We are not being encouraged to give up if we can see something that needs to be said to those in charge. Rather, we are called to patience and gentleness. These characteristics can help to both persuade and break resistance.

Patience

Sometimes in life there are time constraints which call for quick words and decisive action. Yet, this proverb provides a general principle that if there are truths to explain and extra facts to present, we should aim to be patient by taking our time to get to grips with the data and evidence first in order to carefully present our view. We should also be patient in allowing the individual time to understand and consider our point of view.

Gentleness

Sometimes people can seem so inflexible. They won't listen to reason. Unfortunately, we can also be inflexible and reason that the only way to convince someone is to employ a violent offensive to break them down. This proverb tells us that the loudest voice is not always the most fruitful, and the hammer approach can crush rather than encourage flexibility.

✓ Apply

> ❓ *When sharing the gospel with someone, how might this wisdom encourage us to proceed as we seek to convince them of the truth?*

✓ Pray

Pray for your relationship with the "rulers" in your life.

True change can only be brought about in someone's heart by the action of God's Spirit. Pray for any you know who are resistant to the gospel. Ask for the opportunity to deploy patient, gentle words with them.

Priest and King

Hebrews 6:20 told us that Jesus is high priest "in the order of Melchizedek". Who is he? And what does he have to do with our confidence in Christ? Chapter 7 explains…

In Genesis 14, Abraham was coming back from a battle, having rescued his nephew Lot, who had been captured. On the way back, he met Melchizedek and gave him a tenth part of all the spoils. **Read Genesis 14:18-20.** Melchizedek is a historical figure, a real person. But, more importantly, he is also a type of Christ—a figure who points forwards to Jesus and what he would do.

Meet Melchizedek

Read Hebrews 7:1-3

> ❷ *In what ways was Melchizedek like Christ?*

Melchizedek was a real human, and thus would have had a real father and mother (v 3). But the way that Melchizedek is *presented* in Scripture makes it seem that he pops in and pops out without a beginning or an end. So, he seems eternal. Therefore, he is a very effective type of Christ: "resembling the Son of God".

✔ Apply

> ❷ *How does Christ being both priest and King at the same time encourage you today? In what ways do we need Christ to fill each of those roles?*

Two priesthoods

When we think of priests in the Bible, we are generally thinking of the Levitical priesthood. They were descendants of Levi, one of Jacob's twelve sons, and specifically of Aaron, the first priest. But our passage introduces another priesthood: one in the order of Melchizedek, who lived long before Levi and Aaron. And our author is going to make a very simple argument: Melchizedek's priestly order is greater than the Levitical priesthood.

Read Hebrews 7:4-10

> ❷ *The author makes three arguments for the superiority of Melchizedek's priesthood over the Levitical one. What are they?*
> * *v 4-6*
> * *v 6b-7*
> * *v 8*

Why does all this matter? Because Christ is "in the order of Melchizedek" (6:20). Once again, the author is showing us that Christ is superior to all aspects of the old covenant. So the question presented to the readers of Hebrews is: which priesthood would you rather have representing you?

⌃ Pray

Spend some time worshipping Jesus—our King of righteousness and peace, our priest for ever, and the One who is superior in every way to anyone else.

Four more reasons

Our author is not finished comparing priesthoods. In today's passage he lays out four additional reasons why we should always turn to Christ as our true high priest.

Why the change?
Read Hebrews 7:11-12

❷ *Why did we need a new or different priesthood other than the Levitical one (see also 10:1)?*

A change in priesthood implies there will be a *new covenant* that will supersede the old (v 12)—a theme we will revisit in chapter 8.

Better by far

Now that our author has addressed the reason for a new priesthood, he turns to the four features of Christ's priesthood that make it superior.

Read Hebrews 7:13-28

❷ *Reason 1: What was different about the tribe that Jesus came from (v 13-14)? Why is this a good thing, do you think (see Genesis 49:10)?*

In the Old Testament it was not acceptable for the king to make a sacrifice (1 Samuel 13); kings and priests were different offices. But not when it comes to Jesus. He is like no other priest in the Old Testament—he is a priest who can also rule as King.

❷ *Reason 2: How long will Jesus be priest for (Hebrews 7:16-17)? Why does this make him a better priest than the OT ones (v 23-25)?*

How could we have eternal security without an eternal representative? But when it comes to Jesus, you don't have to worry about that. He has no successor because he never dies. Unlike any other priest, Jesus will always, always be there for you. Eternity is a scary thing, but in him we can rest secure.

❷ *Reason 3: How do we know that Jesus will remain our priest? Is there a possibility that God will change the priesthood again (v 20-22)?*

God never said, *I promise you, Aaron will be my priest forever.* He never said, *I swear that the earthly temple system is the way it's going to be forever.* But when he gets to Jesus, he swears an oath. Jesus' priesthood is certain.

❷ *Reason 4: What final difference between Jesus and the Levitical priests does the writer point out (v 26-28)? Why is this good news for us?*

Jesus' perfect life allowed him to do something unthinkable—something no other priest would have ever dreamed of doing: he "offered up himself" (v 27). Now, through him, we can "draw near to God" (v 19).

❷ *Look back over the four reasons. Which are you most encouraged by today?*

With such a Saviour available to us, why turn to anything else? Whatever we are tempted to trust in today other than Jesus, the book of Hebrews bids us let it go. Only Jesus is sufficient to save. Only he is worthy of our hope and trust.

EASTER: Genesis to Jesus

This Easter, in the rest of this issue and the start of the next, we're going to look at the breathtaking story of the cross through the lens of Genesis.

On the road to Emmaus, Jesus meets two of his followers and *radically* transforms their understanding of the Old Testament: "And beginning with Moses and all the Prophets, he explained to them what was said in all the Scriptures concerning himself" (Luke 24:27). Jesus is *everywhere* in the Old Testament, including in the very first book, written by Moses around 1,500 years before the cross. It's our prayer that as you meditate on some of these signposts and shadows of Easter, you'll grasp even more deeply God's gracious character and sovereign plan.

Our Genesis passages will be in chronological order, which means we'll be leaping about the New Testament as we link in with the Easter story and the apostles' explanations of what was going on at the cross. Don't lose heart; rather, be amazed at the beautiful unity of the whole Bible, revealed in God's ever-consistent rescue plan.

A mysterious hint
Read Genesis 1:26-27

> ❷ *What strikes you as strange about v 26?*
> ❷ *What questions about Jesus does this raise?*

Isn't it spectacular? Right here, in the first chapter of the Bible, the Trinity is at work (see also the Spirit in v 2). But this raises some big questions. *How* was Jesus involved in creation? Has he always existed? What is his relationship with God the Father?

An amazing explanation
Read Colossians 1:15-20

> ❷ *How was Jesus involved at creation, and how is he involved now (v 16-17)?*
> ❷ *What does it mean for Jesus to be the image of God (v 15, 19)?*
> ❷ *What are some of the things that Jesus achieved by shedding his blood on the cross (v 18, 20)?*

All things we made by Jesus, for Jesus, and through Jesus. He's the heir of creation—the "firstborn" in the sense that it all belongs to him. We were made in God's image, but Jesus is the *perfect* image of God: God himself clothed in flesh. Through his sacrifice, he has brought peace—peace between us and God, and peace for creation. We, as his people, will see him reign supreme over his universe as the risen, conquering, humble King.

⌃ Pray

The well-known song *The Servant King* contains the line "Hands that flung stars into space, to cruel nails surrendered."

Spend some time responding to God in praise and wonder.

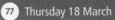
A marriage made in...

Our society often sees marriage as just a nice party followed by a restrictive and dull legal contract. But God's plan is very different.

Adam's bride
Read Genesis 2:18-25

> ❓ *So far, everything in Eden has been "good". What's the problem here (v 18)?*
> ❓ *What is not the solution (v 20)?*
> ❓ *How does Adam react when he sees Eve?*

Adam sings! *At last*, here she is! Eve is *like* Adam, *from* Adam, *for* Adam, but different, complementing him perfectly. It's like a fairy tale: love at first sight. But unlike a fairy tale, this prototype marriage is a shadow of a much deeper spiritual reality.

Christ's bride
Read Ephesians 5:25-32

> ❓ *Paul quotes from our Genesis passage in verse 31. What breathtaking explanation does he give in verse 32?*

Way before Genesis 2, God had already planned out the whole story. He created human marriage to be a beautiful picture of the love Jesus has for his people. Marriage isn't ultimately about us; every marriage is a signpost, whether the participants recognise this or not.

> ❓ *How do we know that Jesus loves the church (v 25)?*
> ❓ *What was the purpose behind this action (v 26-27)?*
> ❓ *What does it look like for a husband to love his wife like this?*

The way a husband models Christ is by seeking his wife's holiness, at the expense even of his own life.

🔼 Pray

Pause to reflect on Jesus' love for you: a love that went to the *greatest* lengths to present you as radiant, without blemish, holy and blameless. Confess ways in which you take this too lightly by toying with sin.

Read Revelation 19:6-9

> ❓ *As all of history reaches its glorious culmination, who is getting married?*

This is where we are heading. We are the bride of Christ. One day, we will stand before him, shining and perfect, all our sin gone for ever because of his sacrifice for us. And Jesus will react like Adam—"*At last!*" All that he has gone through has been to win back his unfaithful bride.

✅ Apply

> ❓ *If you are married, how well are you shadowing the heavenly marriage? Is your marriage centred on helping each other to submit to Christ and grow in love and holiness?*
> ❓ *Whether you are married or not, how does knowing that marriage is a temporary shadow of your future reality help you not to value marriage too highly, or treat it too lightly?*

Temptation

What's the biggest fight you've ever had with temptation? Who won?

Humanity falls

Read Genesis 2:16-17 and 3:1-7

- ❓ *How do both the serpent and Eve twist God's good command?*
- ❓ *The obvious sin is eating the fruit, but what is the sin at the root of this action?*

Adam and Eve fail to trust God's word. They believe there might be something better for them outside of his commands.

Jesus stands

Jesus had already endured a sustained temptation-attack by Satan back at the start of his ministry (see Matthew 4:1-11), as well as the everyday temptations of normal life (Hebrews 4:15). But now, his resolve is tested to the maximum.

Read Matthew 26:47-54

A Roman legion was 6,000 soldiers. So Jesus is saying he could have the backup of 72,000+ angels, if he just asked. A bit more impressive than Peter's sword!

- ❓ *Why does Jesus not give in to this temptation (v 54)?*

Jesus trusts his Father's word. He knows there is nothing better outside of his commands.

Read Matthew 27:38-44

- ❓ *What is Jesus being tempted to do here?*
- ❓ *What would have happened if he'd given in?*

Can you picture it? The eternal King of glory is hanging there, battered and bloodied, gasping for breath, being heartlessly mocked by the very ones he's come to save. It would be *so* easy just to show them—to break out that angel army, to fly down from the cross like superman, to blast them all to smithereens. But he doesn't do any of that. He keeps on obeying his Father, and loving his wayward people, right to the end, because he trusts God's promise of what's coming: "For the joy that was set before him he endured the cross, scorning its shame, and sat down at the right hand of the throne of God." (Hebrews 12:2).

☑ Apply

Jesus has been tempted more severely than any other person because he never gave up. All of us have caved in sooner or later—when temptation has got to a certain point, we've all failed to trust God, failed to rely on him, and lost the battle. We fudge that expenses claim, we make that nasty comment, we watch that porn.

- ❓ *What lies are we believing about Jesus and about our Father when we give in to temptation?*
- ❓ *What promises in God's word can you learn and remind yourself of this week (e.g. 1 Corinthians 10:13: "When you are tempted, he will also provide a way out so that you can endure it")?*

Old Adam/new Adam

We're revisiting the story of the fall from a different angle today, in an attempt to answer the question: how can one man save untold millions?

Our representatives

When our team wins, we shout: "*We* won!" I feel like it's *my* success, in spite of the fact that I wasn't even there. This idea of representation is key to our passage.

Read Romans 5:12-19

❓ *Why does everyone die (v 12)?*
❓ *What's the connection between Adam's sin and our death?*
❓ *What's your reaction to this?*

Note that it's not *Adam sinned; therefore Adam died; therefore all die because all sin like Adam.* No, we all sinned in Adam—Adam's sin is "imputed" to us. And it seems really unfair! We want to represent ourselves, or at least choose our representative. But God chose for us, and that is a really good thing because he is infinitely good and wise. His choice was the best choice.

❓ *How is Adam a pattern of Jesus (v 14)?*

Paul is about to explain that both were the first of a "race" who influenced all those coming afterwards. Whatever they did, good or bad, is imputed to the people they represent. The only way for us to escape Adam's race is to join Jesus' race instead.

Paul then goes on to compare Adam and Christ to show that Christ is better by far:

- v 15: Adam's bad action brings deserved punishment, but Christ's good action brings undeserved reward.

- v 16: Adam's *one* trespass brought condemnation, but our *many* trespasses, instead of bringing lots more condemnation, end in justification—Jesus' gift to us!

- v 17: Adam's trespass caused death to reign, but Jesus' free gift doesn't just cause *life* to reign—it causes *us* to reign! It's more than a reversal!

Finally, Paul finishes his comparison:

- v 18: Adam's trespass ➜ condemnation ➜ for all

- Jesus' righteousness ➜ justification and life ➜ for all

- v 19: Adam's disobedience ➜ many ➜ made sinners

- Jesus' obedience ➜ many ➜ made righteous

❓ *What does this teach us about how we're "made righteous"?*

Just as Adam's sin became our sin, Jesus' righteousness becomes our righteousness, imputed to us. But there's a huge imbalance to the side of grace. When Adam set our sin in motion, we then sinned of our own accord. But when Christ set our righteousness in motion, he then went on to sustain it by his grace—we cannot be righteous by ourselves!

⌃ Pray

Praise Jesus for walking in humanity's shoes so he could represent you instead of Adam.

Be self-controlled

We live in a culture that is given to excess. Whether it's food, drink, media, holidays or a favourite hobby—we binge.

....

Overdosing
Read Proverbs 25:16-17

❷ *What's the instruction of verse 16?*

Honey is sweet and pleasurable, and in the ancient world, a relatively rare find; and yet there is a danger, with pleasurable things, to excessively indulge.

❷ *What things that you find pleasure in do you need to apply this verse to?*

This certainly applies to food, but it is not just food (or drink) that we can indulge in. For example, watching your favourite box set in the evening, playing computer games after work or reading the latest novel before bed? There is often that temptation for just one more chapter, or one more episode—but will you be able to get up for work the next day, or wake up early enough to read your Bible and pray?

The message is simply *know when to stop.*

❷ *How is verse 17 similar yet different from verse 16?*

"Hate", verse 17, is a strong word, but it mirrors the word "vomit" in verse 16. Just like overindulgence can be bad for you, so we can be "too much" for others.

❷ *What might it look like for you to be too much for someone else?*

We are made for relationships, which reflects our relational God, in whose image we were created. And yet we are encouraged to be self-controlled in our relationships and therefore aware of being clingy and overbearing.

⌄ Apply

It may be that there are one or two people who you are especially close to. The wisdom here is not to back away from that close relationship, but to safeguard our relationships by giving space to our friends when they need it—even marriages need this sometimes.

Consequences
Read Proverbs 25:28

❷ *Why should we exercise self-control?*

⌄ Apply

❷ *How can we hurt ourselves if we do not exercise self-control with food, drink, our tongues, sexual desires, money?*
❷ *How can we hurt others with a lack of self-control?*

⌃ Pray

Ask the Lord for discernment to see when a good thing can become harmful and for the strength to stop.

Thank God that there is one friend who will never grow weary of our presence. What a friend we have in Jesus!

The serpent-crusher

Today's passage reveals the first clue about God's rescue plan, which will span millennia.

Sin revealed

Read Genesis 3:8-13

> ❓ *What has happened to Eve and Adam's relationship with God in the aftermath of their sin (v 8, 10)?*
> ❓ *What excuses do they make (v 12, 13)?*

Fear, shame, a desire to hide—Adam and Eve know that they've messed up monumentally. Instead of trusting God's goodness, which he had proved to them abundantly, they trusted Satan's lie that God wasn't good, that he was causing them to miss out. But rather than confessing their sin and asking for forgiveness, they play the blame game.

▾ Apply

It's not fashionable to talk about sin, but it's everywhere.

> ❓ *How do we see these patterns of fear, shame and blame-shifting in our society? In our friends and family?*
> ❓ *What about in you?*
> ❓ *When are you tempted to believe Satan's lie that God isn't good?*

Sin defeated?

Read Genesis 3:14-19

> ❓ *What are the consequences:*
> • *for Eve (v 16)?*
> • *for Adam (v 17-19)?*
> • *for Satan (v 14-15)?*

The curse falls heavily on humanity. God's good gifts of procreation (v 16a), relationships (v 16b), and work (v 17-19) are all infected with pain and difficulty. And worst of all, death enters the world (v 19b). It's devastating.

Yet what is going on in verse 15? In the conflict between the woman's offspring and Satan, both sides receive a crushing blow. But only the man's heel is injured, whereas Satan's *head* is crushed. There's a clear winner. From now on in the Bible narrative, we're on the look-out for this serpent-crusher...

"Since the children have flesh and blood, he too shared in their humanity so that by his death he might break the power of him who holds the power of death—that is, the devil." (Hebrews 2:14)

"The reason the Son of God appeared was to destroy the devil's work." (1 John 3:8)

> ❓ *How does Satan crush the man's heel?*
> ❓ *How does the man crush Satan's head?*
> ❓ *What hope is there here for us who live under the shadow of death?*

▴ Pray

Jesus' death looked like Satan's victory, but was actually his defeat, as Jesus forged a path to resurrection and eternal life. The God who had justly cursed humanity, ultimately bore that curse himself, so that we could live for ever with him in a new, even better Eden. How will you respond?

The cherubim

The terrible consequences of the fall continue, as Adam and Eve are banished from Eden.

Keep out!
Read Genesis 3:8, 21-24

❓ *What does verse 8 tell us about Adam and Eve's pre-fall relationship with God?*

❓ *How does this relationship now change?*

❓ *What is the purpose of the flaming sword and cherubim (a type of angel)?*

Adam and Eve would have lived for ever, in a perfect, intimate relationship with their loving Creator. But their sin breaks this relationship apart: from now on, they will live away from God's presence, and die from disease and decay. The cherubim are a big "KEEP OUT" sign, reminding them that God and eternal life are now inaccessible.

Fast-forward to Moses and the Israelites in the wilderness, and the cherubim appear again, this time as God instructs Moses on how to build the tabernacle: "Make a curtain of blue, purple and scarlet yarn and finely twisted linen, with cherubim woven into it by a skilled worker ... Hang the curtain from the clasps and place the ark of the covenant law behind the curtain. The curtain will separate the Holy Place from the Most Holy Place" (Exodus 26:31-33).

The "Most Holy Place" was the focal point of the tabernacle, and later the temple (see 2 Chronicles 3:14), where God's presence on earth was symbolically focused. It was so holy that only the high priest could enter without dying, and only once a year, on the day of atonement.

❓ *How do the cherubim fulfil the same role here as they did in Eden?*

Come in!
Read Mark 15:37-38

This curtain was no flimsy affair; it was 9cm (3.5 inches) thick—a handbreadth.

❓ *What is the significance of the curtain tearing from top to bottom?*

❓ *Why does the curtain tear at the moment of Jesus' death?*

Since Eden, access to God had been severely limited, for our own protection and was only allowed to special people at special times with special sacrifices. But Jesus' death means we *can* come in to God's presence—anyone, at any time, in any place, right into our Father's arms.

🔼 Pray

Heaven is open to us! Make use of this privilege by praying thankfully through Romans 5:1-2:

"Therefore, since we have been justified through faith, we have peace with God through our Lord Jesus Christ, through whom we have gained access by faith into this grace in which we now stand."

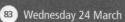
Blood brothers

Eve has a son; could this be the promised serpent-crusher? Alas no—instead he becomes the first murderer…

Abel's blood

Read Genesis 4:1-12

❓ *What's the difference between Cain's offering and Abel's (v 3-4, also v 7a)?*
❓ *How does God respond to each (v 4-5)?*
❓ *Why does Cain kill his brother (v 5-8)?*

It's not altogether clear why God accepted Abel's offering and not Cain's, but Hebrews 11:4 gives us some help:

"By faith Abel brought God a better offering than Cain did. By faith he was commended as righteous, when God spoke well of his offerings. And by faith Abel still speaks, even though he is dead."

Perhaps it's that Abel gave of the best of his flock—the fat portions from the firstborn—whereas there's no mention of Cain giving the firstfruits of his crop. Abel put God first, sacrificing the best to him, but Cain didn't, keeping the best for himself—his motivation was wrong (Genesis 4:7a).

Jesus' blood

Read Hebrews 12:24

❓ *What similarities can you find between Abel and Jesus (see also Hebrews 11:4 above)?*
❓ *What truth did the "blood of Abel" speak?*
❓ *What truth does the blood of Christ speak?*

Jesus was perfectly righteous. He didn't just sacrifice his spotless firstborn lambs—he *was* the spotless firstborn Lamb of all creation (remember Colossians 1:15?). His life was worth more than all other lives put together because he is the infinite God-man. From a purely human viewpoint, he was murdered by his brothers—the Jewish leaders who were jealous of him and feared him. But in reality, he gave his life up voluntarily, opening up the way for sinners to be forgiven once and for all. No more sacrifices were needed:

"But he has appeared once for all at the culmination of the ages to do away with sin by the sacrifice of himself." (Hebrews 9:26)

Abel's blood spoke of guilt and the depths of humanity's sin: it doesn't get much worse than brother murdering brother out of jealousy. Jesus' blood is the blood which ratifies the new covenant (more on this later): it's a symbol of sacrifice, of hope, and of peace.

☑ Apply

❓ *In what ways do you struggle with jealousy? Are you guilty of murdering someone in your heart?*
❓ *Could any feelings of anxiety you have be the result of envy?*

Come to the One who shed his blood for you and repent.

God's wrath

The idea of an angry, punishing God is terribly unpopular today. But if God didn't punish sin, he would be terrifyingly unjust and untrustworthy.

Wrath deserved
Read Genesis 6:5-8

❓ *What are people like?*
❓ *What does God do about it?*
❓ *What does this show us about God's character?*

It's harrowing reading: "*every* inclination ... *only* evil *all* the time" (v 5). And we haven't changed. We deserve destruction. God's perfect justice demands it. Yet Noah was saved, keeping the promise of the serpent-crusher alive...

Wrath delayed
Read Genesis 9:11-13

❓ *What does this show us about God's character?*

Although Noah's descendants will be no better than the people who have just drowned, God makes an everlasting covenant with them, promising never to bring another universal flood. But how is he able to show such grace without compromising his perfect justice? Have his standards suddenly dropped? No; he is being patient with us.

Wrath diverted
Read Matthew 26:38-39

Jesus prays in Gethsemane before he is arrested:

❓ *How is Jesus feeling?*
❓ *What is his attitude to his Father?*

The cup Jesus talks about is the cup of God's wrath (see Jeremiah 25:15). It's God's perfectly just anger at our rebellion against him: God being against us because we have rejected him. Jesus alone, out of every human being ever to exist, did not deserve this wrath. He'd always lived in loving harmony with his Father, enjoying a perfect relationship. Yet he willingly accepts the poisonous cup of wrath, aligning his will with that of his Father, so that we will escape. We sing about this in the hymn "In Christ Alone":

> *Till on that cross as Jesus died,*
> *The wrath of God was satisfied,*
> *For every sin on him was laid,*
> *Here in the death of Christ I live.*

The flood is a shadow of the punishment we all deserve. Either we endure God's wrath ourselves when we die, or we take advantage of God's gracious patience and trust that Jesus was "drowned" in our place.

⌃ Pray

The more we understand God's wrath, the more we will appreciate his love.

Re-read our Matthew passage, thanking Jesus for his astounding sacrifice.

All nations

Abraham is still seen as the father of the Jewish people today. But he's more than that. His story stretches across the next 14 chapters of Genesis, and is full of shadows...

Three promises given

Read Genesis 12:1-4

> ❷ *What does God tell Abram (his name is changed in 17:5) to do (v 1)?*
> ❷ *How does Abram respond (v 4)? Why, do you think?*
> ❷ *What promises does God make to Abram (v 2-3)?*

You may have heard these promises summarised as people, land and blessing. There are lots of brilliant Bible overviews which track these three promises as they are fulfilled throughout Israel's history and on into the New Testament. But notice that there are two parts to this promise. Not only will Abram be blessed, but *all peoples on earth* will be blessed through him! The worldwide curse, which fell in Genesis 3 and spiralled ever downward through chapters 4 – 11, will one day be lifted through Abram's family. These are magnificent promises, received with faith by an elderly man who has no children (see 11:30). Jesus was the great-great-great-times-a-lot-grandson of Abraham.

Three promises fulfilled

Read Matthew 28:19-20

> ❷ *Who are God's people now?*
> ❷ *Where is God's place now? (There's a hint in verse 20.)*
> ❷ *How does the promise of blessing spread to all nations?*

Through Jesus' death and resurrection, the gospel is opened up to the whole world. Being a child of Abraham is no longer contingent on being Jewish. The apostle Paul gives us a brilliant explanation of what it really means in Galatians 3:8: "Scripture foresaw that God would justify the Gentiles by faith, and announced the gospel in advance to Abraham: 'All nations will be blessed through you'."

☑ Apply

God has made us—as God's people, saved by faith in Jesus—to be part of the fulfilment of his promises to Abraham, as we obey Jesus' command to make disciples of all nations: to help others to grow in faith and obedience. But we're not alone—we have Jesus with us by his Holy Spirit!

> ❷ *How are you answering Jesus' call, both at home and by involvement in cross-cultural mission?*

Freeing the captives

To be a captive means to be "imprisoned or confined, having no freedom to choose alternatives or to avoid something".

Lot taken captive

Read Genesis 13:5-13

❓ *Why does Lot choose to go in the direction of Sodom (v 10-11)?*

❓ *What does this say about:*
- *his attitude to Abram (v 9)?*
- *his attitude to God (v 13)?*

This is more than pure pragmatism; at this point Lot is self-seeking and spiritually indifferent. He thinks only of financial gain, with no consideration for what might be best for his uncle or his own soul.

Read Genesis 14:8-16

Sodom is routed, and Lot is taken captive. He's helpless.

❓ *How does Abram respond when he hears the news (v 14)?*

❓ *Is this surprising?*

❓ *Can you think of a way in which Abram is a shadow of Jesus here?*

Lot had done nothing to deserve this rescue. Yet Abram shows compassion, jumping to his aid straight away, and pulls off a decisive and complete victory. Nothing of Lot's is lost.

Everyone taken captive

Read John 8:31-36

❓ *What are the Jews confused about (v 33)?*

❓ *In what way are they desperately in need of being set free (v 34)?*

These Jews are captive to sin but blind to this reality, and so totally unable to be rescued. It's as if Lot hadn't realised that he'd been taken captive by the enemy, and so when Abram turned up with his 318 men, he'd just said *No thanks, I'm fine here.*

⌄ Apply

Look back at the definition of a captive at the top. How does this explain what it means to be a slave to sin? How do we see this in ourselves and in those around us?

❓ *What is the only way to be truly free (v 35-36)?*

❓ *What is the "truth" that Jesus is talking about in verse 32 (see also John 14:6)?*

Jesus is the only answer, the truth, the One who compassionately sets us free. He didn't ride to the rescue in the middle of the night with an army. He died, naked and alone, in untold agony, for us—so that we no longer pay the penalty for our sin, and have the freedom to choose obedience to him instead.

⌃ Pray

Ask God to expose any spiritual blind-spots where you are still behaving like a sin-captive. Give thanks for the freedom Jesus has won for you at the cross, and pray that you would use it to choose obedience. Pray for an opportunity to show compassion to another "captive".

Charcoal kindness

Today's proverb gives a simple but profoundly counter-cultural command.

Love your enemies
Read Proverbs 25:21

❷ *What is your gut reaction if someone hurts or angers you?*
❷ *What is the command in verse 21?*
❷ *Who are your enemies?*

Many of us might not talk about having "enemies", but the proverb recognises that people can wrong us, hurt us and betray us. They make us see red, make our blood boil and push our buttons. And yet the principle here is not that our enemies should simply be on the receiving end of our cooking, but that if we see them in difficulty, we are to alleviate their suffering, want the best for them, serve them and pray for them.

❷ *Consider the following scenarios with a person who has made you see red. How should this command from God move us to act when:*
   • *they suffer a personal tragedy?*
   • *they are being hostile and rude, to your face or behind your back?*
   • *they turn up at your church?*

❷ *Does obeying this command come naturally to you? Why or why not?*

···· TIME OUT ·····

Read Romans 5:9-11

Christians can look back and remember that we were once enemies of God. Our sin that offends God and grieves his heart cut us off from him. But through his grace and mercy he did not leave us to suffer, but came to bring us back to himself through Christ.

Painful kindness
Read Proverbs 25:22

Verse 22 gives us the reason for the command. And it is incredibly loving.

❷ *How would you feel if someone who you hurt did something lovely for you?*

The image of burning coals expresses how our enemies will feel pain—not through our fits of rage or cutting words but through our kindness.

This verse reminds us that our chief concern for people ought to be their eternal salvation. We don't love our enemies for their thanks but so that they would turn to the Lord, who is joyful about anyone leading another to repentance.

⌃ Pray

Read Galatians 5:22-23 and pray that God would grant you the fruit of the Spirit to love your enemies.

A better priesthood (I)

Today it's not Abram who is a shadow of Jesus but the mysterious Melchizedek. We are doing a deeper dig into the passages we looked at a couple of weeks ago.

Melchize-who?

Read Genesis 14:17-20

- ❓ *What are we told about Melchizedek?*
- ❓ *How does he treat Abram?*
- ❓ *How does Abram respond to him?*
- ❓ *Who do you think is "greater": Abram or Melchizedek?*

It's not much to go on, is it? But we do learn that Melchizedek is a king, but also a priest; he blesses Abram, and Abram responds by giving him a tenth of his possessions. As Hebrews 7:7 says, "The lesser is blessed by the greater." Melchizedek is a big deal!

But then we don't hear anything else about him until Psalm 110. This psalm is a stunning prophecy by King David about his greater son, the Messiah; and right in the middle (v 4) we get these strange words: 'The LORD has sworn and will not change his mind: 'You are a priest for ever, in the order of Melchizedek.'"

What's going on? What is the significance of the Messiah being an eternal priest in the order of Melchizedek? We need to go to Hebrews for an explanation...

Compare and contrast

Read Hebrews 7:1-3

- ❓ *What does Melchizedek's name mean (v 2)? How does Jesus fulfil this perfectly?*
- ❓ *How else is Melchizedek like Jesus (v 3)?*

Jesus is our perfect King, the righteous One who brings righteousness to his people and, in doing so, makes peace between humanity and God. He exists from eternity, for eternity, uncreated. (Although Melchizedek was an ordinary human, his family origins and age at death are not mentioned, foreshadowing Jesus' divine nature.)

Next the writer contrasts Melchizedek's priesthood with the Levitical priesthood, instituted when God gave Moses the law back in Exodus. Tomorrow we'll learn more about why Jesus *had* to be our great high priest, but today's passage explains how he *can* be a priest, in spite of the fact that he's from the kingly tribe of Judah instead of the priestly tribe of Levi (see v 14).

Read Hebrews 7:11-22

- ❓ *On what basis were the Old Testament priests appointed (v 16a)?*
- ❓ *On what basis is Jesus a priest (v 16b, 20-22)?*
- ❓ *What could the Levitical priesthood not achieve (v 11)?*
- ❓ *What has Jesus' achieved (v 19)?*

⌄ Apply

Tracing the Christ-shadowing Melchizedek from Genesis, through Psalm 110 and on to Hebrews gives us another little glimpse of God's sovereign plan over history.

- ❓ *How does this encourage you to trust him with your struggles today?*

A better priesthood (II)

Yesterday we saw how Melchizedek's priesthood is a shadow of Jesus' priesthood. But why was this new type of priesthood necessary?

In the Old Testament, the priests offered frequent sacrifices to atone for the sins of the people. This went on and on and on and on—centuries of blood, sweat and tears.

Jesus the priest
Read Hebrews 7:23-28

- ❓ *Compared to the Levitical priesthood, what is better about Jesus' priesthood?*
- ❓ *What is the consequence of this (v 25)?*
- ❓ *How is Jesus different to the priests (v 26)?*
- ❓ *What effect does this have on his sacrifice (v 27)?*

Jesus isn't bogged down in trying to sort out his own sin—he didn't have any, as we've seen. This means that his sacrifice is doubly perfect, because he is both the priest who offers the sacrifice and the sacrifice itself. And we don't need to worry that he's going to die and be replaced by another priest who doesn't remember us—he *always* lives to intercede for us.

> *Before the throne of God above,*
> *I have a strong and perfect plea,*
> *A great high priest whose name is love,*
> *Who ever lives and pleads for me.*

Jesus the sacrifice
Read Hebrews 10:1-4, 8-14

- ❓ *What could the Old Testament sacrifices not achieve on their own (v 1, 4)?*

❓ *How do we know this (v 2-3)?*

These sacrifices were just a shadow of a coming reality (v 1). They reminded the people of their continuing guilt and were never finished—as soon as you'd offered one sacrifice, you'd gone and sinned again and needed another sacrifice.

- ❓ *What is the reality to which the sacrifice ultimately pointed (v 10, 12, 14)?*

> *Because the sinless Saviour died*
> *My sinful soul is counted free*
> *For God the Just is satisfied*
> *To look on him and pardon me.*

🔼 Pray

It's hard to get our heads around: for all of eternity past, God has had a spectacular plan to rescue his wayward creation. And first it involved a very complex sacrificial system, headed by priests, which for 1,500 years reminded the people that they were sinful and that only blood could restore their relationship with God. But this turned out to be only a stop-gap—because the real sacrifice was God himself, the perfect high priest, who offered *himself* as the one-time, humanity-saving sacrifice to end all sacrifices.

As you meditate on what it means for Jesus to be all at once king, priest and sacrifice, praise God for showing you the reality which has come from shadowy Melchizedek.

How to be righteous

Today's passage raises this question: has the way to salvation changed over time? From yesterday's passage, the answer to this question might seem to be yes.

Obedience to the law, with all its priests and sacrifices and rituals, in the Old Testament changes to faith in Jesus in the New Testament. But there's a problem with this. If the way of salvation has changed, from works to faith, then it could change again, and we have no assurance at the cross.

Abram's problem

Read Genesis 15:1-6

❷ *What wonderful assurances does God give Abram (v 1)?*

❷ *Why does Abram struggle to believe this (v 2-3)?*

❷ *How do you think Abram feels about God's promises in verses 4-5?*

❷ *How does Abram respond (v 6)?*

❷ *What effect does this have?*

Many years have passed since God's original promise back in chapter 12, and *still* Abram has no child. Has God forgotten? Or maybe Abram hadn't understood properly? What a relief to hear the promise renewed and clarified: his very own flesh and blood will be his heir. His faith in God's ability and willingness to fulfil this promise puts him in right standing with God. He's not done anything at all.

◣ Apply

❷ *How would you explain what faith is to an unbeliever?*

Abraham's children

In Romans 1 – 3, Paul has explained that no one is righteous; both lawless Gentiles and law-keeping Jews stand condemned as sinners (Romans 3:23), and can only be saved by faith in Jesus' wrath-satisfying death (3:24-25). And it's *always* been this way; Jesus' death works backwards in time as well as forwards, saving all those who trusted in the promise of the serpent-crusher. Paul then uses Abraham as a case study to prove his point: if Abraham, the father of the Jewish nation, was saved by faith, then the way of salvation never has, and never will, change.

Read Romans 4:1-12

❷ *What's the difference between wages and a gift (v 4)?*

❷ *What is saving faith (v 5)?*

❷ *Why is faith itself not a "work"?*

❷ *How does King David's experience back this up (v 6-8)?*

❷ *So who are Abraham's true children (v 11-12)?*

Faith cannot be earned; it's a gift of God's grace—of the God who chooses to cover our sins himself (v 7).

◥ Pray

Ask God for opportunities to share your answer to the "Apply" question above.

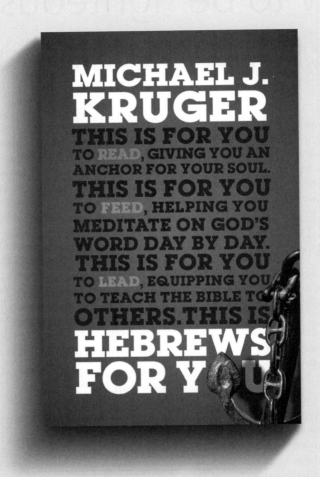

Introduce a friend to

explore

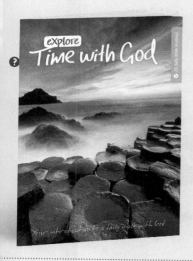

If you're enjoying using *Explore*, why not introduce a friend? *Time with God* is our introduction to daily Bible reading and is a great way to get started with a regular time with God. It includes 28 daily readings along with articles, advice and practical tips on how to apply what the passage teaches.

Why not order a copy for someone you would like to encourage?

Coming up next...

- Genesis and Easter
  with Anna Marsh and Paul Jump

- Hebrews *with Michael Kruger
  and Katy Morgan*

- Proverbs
  with Kathleen Nielsen

- 2 Chronicles
  with Tim Thornborough

Don't miss your copy. Contact your local Christian bookshop or church agent, or visit:

K & Europe: thegoodbook.co.uk
fo@thegoodbook.co.uk
l: 0333 123 0880

orth America: thegoodbook.com
fo@thegoodbook.com
l: 866 244 2165

Australia: thegoodbook.com.au
info@thegoodbook.com.au
Tel: (02) 9564 3555

India: thegoodbook.co.in
info@thegoodbook.co.in
Tel: (+44) 0333 123 0880

Join the *explore* community

The *Explore* Facebook group is a community of people who use *Explore* to study the Bible each day.

This is the place to share your thoughts, questions, encouragements and prayers as you read *Explore*, and interact with other readers, as well as contributors, from around the world. No questions are too simple or too difficult to ask.

JOIN NOW:
facebook.com/groups/tgbc.explore